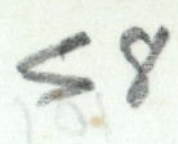

AF553705

ACHIEVEMENT IN SCIENCE

DIGUMARTI BHASKARA RAO
DIGUMARTI PUSHPA LATHA

DISCOVERY PUBLISHING HOUSE
NEW DELHI—110 002

First Published - 1995

Reprinted - 2018

ISBN: 978-81-7141-280-8

Achievement in Science

Published by:

DISCOVERY PUBLISHING HOUSE PVT. LTD.

4383/4B, Ansari Road, Darya Ganj
New Delhi-110 002 (India)
Phone: +91-11-23279245, 43596064-65
Fax: +91-11-23253475
E-mail: discoverypublishinghouse@gmail.com
sales@discoverypublishinggroup.com
web: www.discoverypublishinggroup.com

Printed at:
Infinity Imaging Systems
Delhi

Preface

Science has become an integral part of mankind. We cannot live luxuriously without science and its application. We can not even imagine a world without the involvement of science. Identifying the importance of science in human life and societal development, it has been made a compulsory subject in school education and an elective subject at +2 level who wish to pursue science, engineering and technology courses.

The students of +2 level have to understand well the science either to use it in their daily life or to become professionals in science and technology. Their scientific knowledge can be measured through their achievement in science. This achievement level of science students helps the educationists to classify the students according to their ability in science and to provide essential guidance and counselling.

Considering the above aspects, the achievement of +2 science students has been measured by this study. This study reveals that the achievement of +2 students is very high. The residential type of educational system has played a commendable role in improving the students' achievement in science.

To enhance the academic achievement in our educational institutions, we must provide good physical facilities, we must chose efficient teachers, we must use appropriate teaching techniques, we must extensively involve the students in learning, we must associate our educational institutions with the community resources, and above all, we must manage the campuses as temples of learning.

Dr. D. Bhaskara Rao
Mrs. D. Pushpa Latha

Acknowledgements

We are grateful to the science educators who have contributed their thought and vision in preparing this book. Their perceptions and contributions added flesh and blood to our ideas.

We are thankful to Prof. Marlow Ediger, Northeast Missouri State University, Kirksville, U.S.A., Prof. Willard J. Jacobson, Teachers College, Columbia University, U.S.A., Prof. Skip Hills, Queen's University, Canada; Prof. Brian McAndrews, Queen's University, Canada; Prof. Evelin Witruk, University of Leipzig, Germany; Prof. J. Preston Prather, University of Virginia, U.S.A.; Prof. Antonia Bettencourt, Michigan State University, U.S.A. and Prof. Kiyoshi Amano, Chou University, Japan for supporting our work through their literature.

We are thankful to Mr. P. Koteswara Rao, Mr. M. Nageswara Rao, Dr. B.K. Manmohan Singh, Dr. L. Rathaiah, Dr. K.R.S. Sambasiva Rao, Mr. V. Venkateswara Rao, Mrs. D. Vijaya Lakshmi, Mr. G. Nageswara Rao and Mr. M. Janardhana Rao for their manual and material help.

We extend our thanks to the principals of the colleges for giving us the required data to measure the achievement of +2 students in science.

Bhaskara Rao
Pushpa Latha

Contents

Introduction

> Science is no longer the quintessence of knowledge and of what is worth knowing, but a way. It is a way of penetrating into unexplored and unmastered realms.

From its inception in the early years of ancient Greek civilization, science has been devoted to the quest for a better understanding of nature. Throughout most of history, however, scientific inquiry was neither widely practiced nor perceived as a potential source of human benefit. Rather, it was more or less an elite, intellectual activity indulged in by a few people whose social position provided the learning and leisure time for such pursuits. That perception prevailed until the latter part of the Renaissance, when a revolutionary new concept of the nature and social relevance of science emerged. That era of history is distinguished as "The Scientific Revolution," which is generally dated from the early 1500s to the publication of Isaac Newton's sweeping theory of nature around 1700A.D.

During that brief period, a concept of natural phenomena developed that resulted in a new scientific outlook and a fundamental redefinition of what constitutes meaningful scientific inquiry. At the same time, an equally revolutionary re-interpretation of the term "history" occurred that drastically changed the cultural concept of what constitutes meaningful historical research. The cultural flux that accompanied these changes generated an unprecedented awareness of a potential social utility of science that changed the concept of human destiny, inspired the invention of public science education, and ushered in the modern era of applied science. Within the context of earlier concepts of science, however, the idea of public science education as it is conceived today would have met with little interest or support.

The history of science is rooted in the Golden Age of Greek philosophy, which probably began around 700–600 B.C. and culminated in the Aristotelian era three centuries later. During that relatively brief time, science was born of the philosophers' quest to comprehend the orderly workings of a systematic and predictable universe formed by natural processes. As a result of its origins in philosophy, scientific inquiry was commonly referred to as "natural philosophy".

Before the era of Greek natural philosophy, the notion of objective scientific inquiry would have been generally meaningless. Natural phenomena were perceived as *Thous* rather than objective *its*. "Primitive thought naturally recognized the relationship of cause and effect" (Frankfort *et al.*, 1946), but it was conceived as a personal interaction with the phenomenal world. Some ancient thinkers saw the world around them in terms of gods, and others in terms of natural personages. The stone that hurt the foot that stumbled on it, the wind that blew off a hat, and other occurrences were not perceived as person-object encounters with a very real, live presence of Nature.

Most ancient societies felt a need to live in harmony with the *Thous* that constituted their environs. Every natural occurrence was considered a sign, and insight into the environment was believed to be open to perceptive persons who could sense the subjective meaning of natural events. Within this pragmatic epistemological framework, nature observation was the primary source of information for survival. Elaborate systems were developed for collecting data on a variety of recurrent phenomena such as the periodic fluctuations of the flow of the Nile River, the seasons of the year, the apparent motion of the stars, volcanic eruptions, and the ocean tides.

The resultant data indicated a high degree of predictability, but the lack of a concept of *natural order* precluded the notion that such events might be reliably predicted. The causes of natural events were conceived in terms of worldly powers with which people "were forced to wrestle, and which they sought to propitiate" (Toulmin and Goodfield, 1962). A *Thou* believed to be unique and could be known "only in so far as it reveals itself" (Frankfort, et al., 1946). Tabulation of observational data may reveal a natural history of repetitive patterns; but if Nature could keep secrets, there would always be room for surprise. Ancient history is replete with accounts of humanity's efforts, frequently of ritualistic nature, to cope with an environment conceived in terms of a host of capricious, potentially malevolent *Thous.*

The ancient Egyptians, for example, knew what to expect of the Nile River on the basis of their vast tabulations; but the river might *choose* to behave differently the next time for any sort of personal reason. If the river failed to rise on schedule "it has *refused* to rise" (Frankfort, et al., 1946), possibly because it was offended by those whose needs it affected. In an effort to guard against offending or otherwise alienating a potentially malevolent local natural power, many ancient societies selected and supported individuals whose primary social function was the interpretation of natural phenomena and propitiation. The interpreters, generally called priests, played a major role in the direction of ancient governments; and some of the more successful were enthroned as priest-kings.

Interpretations of meanings of natural events contributed to a growing body of behavioural norms intended to gain the good will of the natural forces that affected their environment. The well-being of society required that those social values be communicated to other generations; and this problem was handled by what is perhaps the oldest strategy of formal, public education: Mythology. Through the facility of mythology, Wells (1961) concluded, a person could be trained to suppress specific attitudes or actions for the common good. Nature was conceived on a personal basis; and within that world view, the idea of an impersonal, natural order that could explain events in terms of general principles or laws was inconceivable. The scientific explanation of the Nile River's flow as related to remote meteoric events, for example, would have been considered *unmythical* and therefore as unsatisfactory to an ancient Egyptian priest as a mythological interpretation would be to a modern scientist.

Temple cultures developed around the priesthood as it gained power, and city states eventually formed around the temples. Ultimately, the Agean priest-kings of ancient Egypt and Mesopotamia established empires among the scattered city states; and the priesthood characterized one of humanity's earliest attempts toward social stability beyond the tribal form of leadership. The priestly government, however, lacked the strength of defend the scattered city states against repeated assaults of invaders from the North.

Nomadic Greek tribes moved southward into the Balkan peninsula between 1,000 and 800 B.C. These tribes "conquered and largely destroyed the civilization that preceded their arrival; (and) upon its ashes they built a civilization of their own (Wells, 1961). The conquered empires had long traditions of mythopoeic thought and relatively centralized rule through the priests. The early Greeks, however, had a quite different set of social values dictated by the sense of individuality and independence characteristic of its prehistoric nomadic heritage. Through the genius of epic poets such as Homer, the Greeks had maintained their own mythology, but it represented a radically different world view from that of their new Egyptian and Mesopotamian neighbors. That different perspective, along with the Greek sense of independence, was to play an important role in the development of science.

The mythical traditions of the Greeks' predecessors were serious attempts to understand nature, but they were developed without the subject-object correlation characteristic of scientific thought. The systematic collection of large amounts of information through astronomical and fluvial studies, for example, produced an excellent observational data base; but the disciplined collection and study of data does not necessarily constitute scientific inquiry. Rather, scientific inquiry "requires some set of assumptions to tell the researcher what data to collect and then how to interpret it" (Brown, 1977). However, such a set of assumptions would have been unacceptable to most pre-Greek cultures. For ancient humanity, Frankfort et al. (1946) observed, mythical representations of nature were not subject to critical analysis and development. Rather, mythological interpretations were built upon the assumption that "one cannot argue about a revelation; it transcends reason". That which Nature had voluntarily revealed to perceptive viewers was considered appropriate knowledge; but prying into the secrets of nature was inappropriate because it might offend some sensitive

Thou, godly or otherwise. The concept of intellectually conceived theories to guide the collection and interpretation of data would have been an anathema under those conditions. Within the mythopoeic world view, it would have been considered a dangerous enterprise.

As the early Greeks saw it, however, there was no cause for concern. Like other civilizations in early antiquity, they had strong religious traditions; "and the Gods of Olympus were not very different from contemporary Gods in the Middle East" (Toulmin and Goodfield, 1961). However, Wells (1961) reported, there was no record of either priest-kings or a temple-state era in the Greek civilization. There was a vaguely defined stratification of Greek society; but whenever a major leader was needed, as in time of warfare, a temporary commander was chosen, generally by democratic processes, as a "leader among his equals". In ancient Greece, there was no priestly tradition to suggest external guidelines for what might be appropriate conduct, intellectual, governmental, or otherwise.

The spirit of independence that fostered the development of ancient science is clearly reflected in Greek mythology. In the poetic account of origins written by Hesiod (sometime in the eighth century B.C.), gods and humans sprang from the same parents : Sky and Earth (Frankfort, *et al.*, 1946). Similarly, Thales contended that "cosmos and earth had been formed by a natural process" (Goldstein, 1980). Claiming common ancestry with the gods, the ancient Greeks approached questions of naturalistic enquiry with much less reserve than their peers; and it was in this unrestrained intellectual arena that the concept of *theory* was invented.

Their sense of secular freedom and personal independence enabled the ancient natural philosophers to "look at the world in cheerful reliance on their senses, in easy companionship with the gods" (Goldstein, 1980). Their religious beliefs did not hamper their quest for a rational explanation of the cosmos, and "their curiosity was as live as it was unhampered by dogma" (Frankfort et al., 1946). As nomads, they had sensed that their own destiny was largely dependent upon their own physical and intellectual resourcefulness. The risk of accepting information from any source without careful examination was a sensitive issue, and they placed much emphasis on the value of critical analysis to weigh their interpretations. As a result, their scientific speculations were deeply rooted in a highly systematic system of logic.

"We may think of Greek science as the first systematic and inclusive attempt to explain the entire natural cosmos" (Goldstein, 1989). Like their neighbors to the East, the ancient Greek philosophers sensed as apparent cause-effect relationship in the events around them, but they did not conceive cause as originating in incomprehensible mythological personages. After all, in the Greek world view, both people and gods lived among natural phenomena that could be described in terms of general relationships. For them there was more to nature than the emotions generated by their encounters with natural events. Things had properties and values independent of human experience.

Rather than seeking the subjective meanings of experiences, the Greeks sought rational explanations in the sense of comprehensible *first-causes* or sustaining principles that were subject to critical intellectual judgement. Though they associated gods with all things, they attempted "to understand the coherence of the *things*" (Frankfort, *et al.*, 1946). This bold new perspective laid the basis for objective observations and theoretical speculations of natural relationships.

> This change of viewpoint is breath-taking. It transfers the problems of (humanity) in nature from the realm of faith and poetic intuition to the intellectual sphere.....These men proceeded, with preposterous boldness or an entirely unproven assumption. They held that the universe is an intelligible whole In other words, they presumed that a single order underlies the chaos of our perceptions and, furthermore, that we are able to comprehend that order.

Implicit in that viewpoint is a metaphysical question of fundamental importance for the philosopher of science and scientist alike: "What must the world be like in order that man may know it ?" (Kuhn, 1970). That question, which may be appropriately called the *First Problem of Science*, "is as old as science itself, and it remains unanswered". Clearly, that fact does not prescribe scientific inquiry, as the history of science indicates, and it certainly did not intimidate the early Greeks. "Neither their basic assumption—that the world is an intelligible whole—nor.......any of their other theses can be proved by logic or by experiment or by observation," Frankfort, *et al.* (1946) concluded; but "with conviction they propounded theories which resulted from intuitive insight and which were elaborated by deductive reasoning". Reason, for the ancient Greeks, was the highest authority.

The early Greek scientist or natural philosophers—Toulmin and Goodfield (1961) declared the terms synonymous—believed that natural phenomena could be explained in terms of an intellectual *natural order* that would ensue independently of an observer. In their search for the principles of that order, they raised the study of nature "from a level of scattered empirical observations to the order of a consistent natural philosophy" (Goldstein, 1980). "The Greeks were the effective forerunners of modern science, not in their particular answers and theories, but rather in the new *questions* they put into circulation.......To them belongs the glory of having invented the very idea of a scientific theory" (Toulmin and Goodfield, 1961). For their concept of natural order, their perception of objectivity in the relation of cause and effect, and the invention of theory, the ancient Greek philosophers deserve the honor of recognition for the *invention of science.*

It is important to note, however, that even in the heyday of Greek natural philosophy, science was never a widespread activity; and it was not perceived as having practical social utility. Rather, scientific inquiry was purely intellectual activity indulged in by only a few Greeks, and they were generally "men of leisure" (Toulmin and Goodfield, 1961).

> Critical speculation about the powers of Nature was in fact an unpopular, minority activity even in Athens.........all in all, in the five centuries following 650BC, the number of people who contributed actively to "Greek Science" can have been only a few dozen; and the number of their compatriots who read or listened to their teachings with any real understanding probably amounted to no more that a few hundred.

Apparently, unlike their mythopoeic predecessors, the ancien Greeks saw no need to promote a public knowledge of the fruits of their naturalistic speculation. The concept of public science education that emerged nearly 2,000 years later, in the latter part of the Renaissance, would have been considered meaningless in the ancient Greek culture.

The conditions that nurtured the development of ancient science continued into the early years of the Hellenistic culture, which grew from the consolidation of the previously independent Greek city-states into the empire of Philip of Macedonia (382-336 B.C) and his son Alexander the Great (356-323 B.C.). Aristotle (384-322B.C.) had been Alexander's teacher. From that unique position at the interface of the Greek and Hellenistic cultures, Aristotle projected the powerful heritage of Greek natural philosophy into the centrally governed, cosmopolitan civilization that characterized the Alexandrian empire. "On the face of it," Toulmin and Goodfield (1961) said, "there was no reason why Greek science should not expand to embrace all aspects of the natural world and all sorts of problems".

> After 250 B.C. the intellectual Centre of the Greek world shifted to Alexandria, and there the opportunities for scientific work were in many ways more favorable than they had been earlier in Athens. Yet science gradually lost its momentum, and scientists lost faith in their methods. New sorts of questions were rarely asked; urgent but intractable problems were shelved.

The crucial problem, Santillana (1961) declared, was "the lack of an applied science". The problem stated by Santillana highlights an obscure but important distinction between ancient and modern science. "'Nature,' Aristotle declared, 'refuses to be badly administered'". Greek science assumed a *Teleological* universe wherein "everything in nature has a purpose and is animated by a soul fitted to its purpose" (Toulmin and Goodfield, 1961). In that cosmology, the universe was linked into a systematic, operational unity in which all things were essentially interrelated. The goal of Greek science was "an intellectual grasp based not just on bare theories, but on a new vision of nature—a new harmony of the reason and the senses".

"The relationship of Greek thought to nature remains fundamentally different from ours : it is not a search for the point of attack from which to attempt a break-through, but it was inconceivable that science could be systematically applied or made to behave for social benefit. The Greeks conceived an operable universe; but it was operated from a sphere far above the realm of social necessity, with each entity functioning according to a purposive, natural, *Soul.* Humanity was a part of nature; and, nature, in the Greek system, simply could not be subverted to the purposes of one of its parts.

Perhaps largely because of the Greeks' world view, technology and science developed independently of each other. Technological and engineering know-how were valued for the building of roads, cities, aqueducts, and weapons. The craft of mixing or rearranging stones, clays, metals, and liquids was one thing—but the idea of exploiting the very principles of nature to effect the purposes of society was unthinkable. Greek scientists occasionally cited the ancient crafts as evidence for their theories, Toulmin and Goodfield (1962) noted, but there was no direct relationship of ancient science and technology. Greek philosophers sought to understand the order of nature, but not for purposes of reordering nature. If nature were administered from a higher order as the Aristotelians presupposed, then one could "hardly think of questioning them by way of an experiment" (Santillana, 1961)

The modern science concepts of non-purposive laws of nature, experimental scientific methodology, and application of science to the resolution of societal problems were unknown in ancient science. Consequently, the idea that science might significantly effect the destiny of society was not a conceivable option for dealing with the turbulent social conditions associated with the Alexandrian and Roman empires. "Science ......was not undertaken with any technological end in view" (Toulmin and Goodfield, 1961). The inventions of Archimedes (287—212 B.C.) were notable exceptions but, according to the Greek biographer Plutarch, Archimedes and his peers perceived such machines "not as matters of any importance but as mere amusements in geometry" (Santillana, 1961). Three centuries later, Heron of Alexandria established a school of engineering and systematically applied his scientific knowledge to the invention of complex steam and water-driven machines. He openly advocated the practical uses of such machines, but his work drew little attention. His creations, like those of Archimedes, were perceived as toys for the entertainment and edification of aristocrats and rulers.

Natural philosophy, and philosophy in general, had been on the defensive in ancient Rome from about 100 B.C. Most of the Romans' attention was focused on technological and religious concerns, according to Toulmin and Goodfield (1961), and scientific speculation was not perceived as necessary to either enterprise. Had the concept of a social utility of science occurred in the Golden Age of Natural Philosophy, or even during the later Hellenistic era, the destinies of ancient science and society might have been dramatically different. However, only conjecture can issue from consideration of the potential of science for the ancient Greco-Roman civilization. Some day, historians can reveal with authority the worth of applied science for the modern world, but never for antiquity.

Science was not rejected as an option by ancient society. Rather science simply was never recognized as possessing possible social significance. The prevailing world view would not accommodate such an idea. It is as inappropriate to fault ancient scientists for not attempting to apply their scientific knowledge to pressing social problems of their time as it would be decry a modern scientist's lack of interest in applying science to basic religious problems. Within the context of their relative traditions, neither consideration is an appropriate scientific objective. Consequently, the modern concept of public science education was unheard of and, if known, would have been considered absurd in ancient Greek and Roman societies.

Greek science, however, did not perish. Largely due to the influence of Alexander's teacher, Aristotle, natural philosophy was established and subsidized as a component of the program of the Alexandrian museum and library (Toulmin and Goodfield, 1961). This centralization of natural philosophy in that great center of learning established an ancient equivalent of a modern think-tank, but without a technology for communicating with the rest of the world. The Alexandrian museum and library "were a centre of light", Wells (1961) observed, "but it was light in a dark lantern hidden from the general world". Greek science was institutionalized, respectably cloistered in a splendid, isolated, self-nurturing environment. It buttered no bread for a practical society preoccupied with building a stable socio-political system. Still it was subsidized, or kept, in case if could be morally uplifting or entertaining to the ruling class. Ancient science was thus established as the exclusive domain of "a new type of human being, ...the Scholarly Man" (Wells, 1961). So encumbered, the Golden Age of Natural Philosophy came to an end.

The study of science is a human pursuit which is thoroughly international in essence and import. Though it has become a tradition to believe that science and other strands of human culture have their origin in the eastern outposts of the Greek confederation yet to those, who have even a little insight into the vital and prominent role played by the Aryan scientists, the truth of Manu about the cultural heritage of India will need no emphasis. Manu proclaimed that "from a Brahmana, born in this country, let all men on earth learn their several usages". The great sage Yajnyavalka of the time of King Janaka declared that "the real purpose of life lies in the scientific investigation of this universe".

Max-Mueller said in *India, what can it teach us*, "If I were asked under what sky the human mind has most fully developed some of its choicest gifts, has most deeply pondered on the greatest problems of life and has found solutions of some of them which deserve the attention even of those who have studied Plato and Kant, I should point to India".

Lenin not only asked the Russian intellectuals to study the Ancient Indian heritage of knowledge, but in his enthusiasm, he asked them to go to the Russian working class and explain it to them. In his conversation with S.F. Oldenburg, Lenin said, "Well, there is your subject. It seems far away. Yet it is close. Go to the masses, to the workers and tell them about the history of India.......and see how they will respond to it. And you yourself.....draw inspiration from it for fresh research, work and study of great scientific importance".

Laplace said,"How grateful we should be to the Hindus who discovered this decimal system that did not occur to the minds of such mighty mathematicians as Archimedes and Apollonius."

Albert Einstein, who is regarded as the greatest scientist of the twentieth century once said, "we owe a lot to Indians, who taught us how to count, without which no worthwhile scientific discovery could have been made".

According to Goldstucker, "The most scientific grammar that the world has ever produced with its alphabet based on thoroughly phonetic principles was composed in India."

Professor Mecdonell's tribute is significant : "We Europeans......2500 years later and in a scientific age, still employ an alphabet which is not only inadequate to represent all the sounds of our language, but even preserves the random order in which vowels and consonants are jumbled up as they were in the Greek adaptation of the primitive arrangement of 3000 years ago". He further says, "In science too, the debt of Europe to India has been considerable. There is, in the first place, the great fact that the Indians invented the numerical figures, used all over the world. The influence which the decimal system of reckoning, dependent on those figures has had, not only on mathematics but on the progress of civilization in general, can hardly be over-estimated. During the eighth and ninth centuries, the Indians became the teachers, in arithmetic and algebra, of the Arabs and through them of the nations of the West."

British scientist-cum-historian, J.D. Bernal writes in *Science in History* : "There was also, and this is of greatest importance for the whole world, a new development of science, particularly mathematics and astronomy associated with the names of the two, Aryabhata and Varahamihira in the fifth century, and with Brahmagupta in the seventh..... A decisive new development was made there about this time: the perfection of a number system with place value notation and a zero...... The Arabs also incorporated the work of a series of Indian mathematicians on the means of dealing with unknown quantities which we call algebra".

John Bardeen of the University of Illinois, winner of 1956 and 1972 Nobel Prizes, while (January 9, 1977) receiving Delhi University's Hon. D.Sc. said, "The world has a lot to learn from India and its sages, especially since fossil fuels, responsible for the western world's recent prosperity, were likely to be exhausted by the end of the century. Prosperous nations will have to learn to change their life-styles as a result".

These quotations amply corroborate the supremacy of Indian thought (*Bhartiya Darshan*).

As early as when the Greeks had just begun to develop philosophical thinking, history has on record the details of a discussion between the Greek King Milind and the Buddhist philosopher Nagasena to whom King went for enlightenment. The fact that the king finally took to Buddhism itself confirms the indisputable fact that knowledge did not flow from Greece to India. Indian thought had clearly begun to enlighten the Western thinkers centuries before the dawn of the Christian era. Long before the invasion of Alexander, from 500 B.C. onwards, exchange of knowledge was already established between the Hindus and the Greeks. This was a period when Kuru ruled over Kambhoj, which is the present Afghanistan and Iran.

It is for the West to answer the mystery as to why King Clement of Alexandria called the Greek philosopher and mathematician Pythagoras (570–497 B.C.) as 'the pupil of a Brahmin'? Pythagoras was well known to the world for his ascetic life and vegetarianism which he enthusiastically preached in the West. The theorem which goes in his name, was known in India at least two centuries before his birth. The theorem had found mention at several places in the *Satapatha Brahmana and Baudhayana Sulbasutra*. Every Brahmin was supposed to know the theorem as a part of *Yajna* for making the *vedi*. There is every chance that Pythagoras might have learnt this theorem from Indians. In any way, he can't be credited with the originality of the theorem.

It is again for the West to answer why physicians were called to Persia about 200 A.D. to give anesthesia for a painless operation? Why, at a time, when Indians were supposedly just learning from Greeks, were the great works on chemistry of Nagarjuna and many others being enthusiastically translated into Chinese and other foreign languages. It is a fact recorded by the Ancient Greeks who came to India before the Christian era that the medical science in India was highly developed and that the Indian doctors were praised for their specialized knowledge of the treatment of poisons etc. It is also a well known fact that, later, when *Ayurveda* was translated into the Latin language, the translator could not translate the Sanskrit word 'Arugna phuphus Murmur' meaning the instrument of stethoscope which was used by physicians in India. He translated it in Latin as, "Healthy Vascicular Murmur" retaining the original Sanskrit word 'Murmur' which exists in the English language even today in its original form.

Also *Vishnu Purana* says that at the time of *Sambh* (*i.e.* at the time of *Mahabharata*), the Brahmins of regions outside India and particularly the whole of Central and West Asia knew the four *Vedas*, in a slightly distorted form. Since the originals were available in India, *so the migration must have taken place from India to the West as against the general theory of the Aryans branching off to India.*

If all thinking in India begins after Christ when Greek knowledge is supposed to have reached India, how is one to explain the composition of the *Geeta*, which is accepted, even by Western scholars, to be not later than the fourth century B.C.? It would be relevant to quote Marxist philosopher Bani Despande in *The*

Universe of Vedanta as saying, "It is my firm opinion that *Geeta*, as the quinstessence of the ancient Vedanta philosophy is based on the doctrine of dialectics which was unknown to the West until Marx could explain it in the nineteenth century and its higher development is still unknown in the twentieth century." Also if *Shankhya* and *Yoga* were developed after Christ, by Kapila Muni, on the basis of knowledge derived from Greek thinkers, how could Krishna say in the Geeta that he was the incarnation of Kapila Muni :

(सिद्धानां कपिलो मुनि: I, Geeta—10-26, Shanti—340-60). This exposes the ridiculous Western line of thinking that Kapila Muni lived after Pythagoras.

Jean Filliozat, the eminent French Indologist said, "The greatest historians of science have not always escaped from the inconvenience of knowing only one side of the matter. Paul Tannery, famous for his studies on ancient mathematics, is an example. We know that the trigonometric—sine is not mentioned by Greek mathematicians and astronomers; that it was used in India from the Gupta period onwards, that the *Surya-Siddhanta* gives a table of sines, that the Arab astronomers knew them from their Indian contacts and passed them on to Europe in the twelfth century, when the work of Al-Battani (A.D.858-929) known as Albategnius in Medieval Europe, was translated into Latin......... But Paul Tannery, persuaded that the Indians could not have made any mathematical inventions, preferred to assume that the Indians knew sines was sufficient proof that they must have heard about them from the Greeks....... If this is the way we are to argue, there was never any science other than Greek science, and the questions whether science has any origin other than the Greek science, and the questions whether science has any origin other than the Greek 'miracle' is solved in advance".

Sabokht, a Syrian priest-astronomer of the seventh century A.D. wrote,"I shall now speak of the knowledge of the Hindus, of their subtle discoveries in the science of astronomy—discoveries even more ingenious than those of the Greeks and the Babylonians, of their method of calculation which no word can praise strongly enough, I mean the system using nine symbols. If these things were known to the people who think that they alone have mastered the sciences because they speak Greek, they would perhaps be convinced though a little late in the day that other folk, not only Greeks, but men of a different tongue know something as well as they".

The famous Chinese scholar Fa-hien who came to India in search of knowledge, spent about 10 years (A.D.401–410) in the Gupta empire. His extensive report includes references to the great centres of learning, liberal governments and their patronage of education, instances of inter-caste marriages, abundance of hospitals, a taxing system based on the richness of the locality, the importance of the Vaisya (merchants) community, and above all an effective system of law and order.

Indian sciences were transmitted to the Arab countries through translations of Sanskrit literature into Arabic, or indirectly from Sanskrit to Persian and then Arabic. It is said that during the eighth century, when Sindh was under the actual control of the Caliph Mansur (A.D.753–774), scholars from that part of India went to Baghdad and took with them the words of Brahmagupta. Those works are translated by Arab scholars with the help of Sanskrit *pundits*. It is through them that the Arabs first became acquainted with Indian mathematics and astronomy. This knowledge was further transmitted through the Arabs to the nations of the West.

The isolation of the intellectual community eventually took its toll, and the interests of Alexandrian philosophers turned inward from the remote world of nature toward theological and occult issues that concerned their patrons. Throughout the early years of Greek thought, humanity had been perceived as an integral part of nature. Now the tie was severed, and the natural philosopher "consoled himself by saying in very beautiful and elaborate forms that the world was illusion and that there was in him something quintessential and sublime, outside and above the world" (Wells, 1961). Thus fell the early Greeks' confidence in the intelligibility of nature and, along with it, the basis of future development in Greek science. By time to Ptolemy (about 150A.D.), "cosmology, physics, and mathematical astronomy, brought together by Aristotle, had fallen apart again; and the science of the sky had become once more only a collection of mathematical techniques" (Toulmin and Goodfield, 1961). Basic questions about the nature of causes of things were simply ignored in Ptolemy's theory of the universe. Ptolemy's system, however, could provide an accurate description and prediction of astronomical events; and it was widely acclaimed for these purposes. Apparently, ancient society had come full circle and was once again satisfied with the predictive power of natural history—as people had been long before the invention of science. As the fascination with an explanation of *why* things happened waned, the essence of Greek science disappeared from the scene.

Failing confidence in human resourcefulness ultimately set the stage for the onset of the Middle Ages. As marauding barbarian tribes continued to test the Roman Empire's borders, the initial confidence in society's ability to maintain socio-political stability dwindled. A subsequent monarchy failed to produce the desired social stability, and a stronger form of military rule was sought. Military government also proved inadequate; and finally, divinity was ascribed to the monarch, or Caesar, who was thereby expected to outperform a mere human being. Even a divine ruler was not enough to provide protection from external invasion, however; and a supernatural liaison was effected in an effort to save the State. In 325 A.D., Christianity was established as the official state religion of the Roman Empire; but even this new approach was insufficient to unify a disillusioned citizenry.

Ancient Western Civilizations finally succumbed to a long series of invasions by the Germanic, Oriental, and Arabic tribes that swarmed its borders. "The breakdown of ancient civilization had played brutal havoc with the cosmic imagination of Western man", Goldstein (1980) declared. By about 450 A.D. a civilization which was once confident of its ability to sense its nature and to establish a stable society had relinquished control of all human affairs—intellectual, political, or otherwise—to non-sensible, supernatural authority. The atmosphere in Rome became so intolerant, Toulmin and Goodfield (1961) note, until "unorthodox views ran the risk of condemnation.......as treason". The center of natural philosophy migrated Eastward across the frontiers into Persia and beyond as philosophers sought "a more favorable atmosphere for their work". Science and the physical world were largely forgotten in most of Europe as medieval society reckoned with theocratic rule. With this, systematic naturalistic inquiry faded from Western tradition, and science became a non-entity in the land of its creation.

All was not lost for science in the Middle Ages, however. An interest in nature was maintained in the Middle-Eastern intellectual centers to which many natural philosophers had migrated. As they traveled Eastward seeking refuge for their ideas in the relative intellectual freedom of Persia, many natural philosophers carried with them manuscripts of the works of Aristotle, Archimedes, and others from the prime of Greek science. Early in seventh century AD, the Middle East was overrun by the emerging Muslim Empire, a theocracy based on the new religion of Islam founded in Arabia around 630 A.D. Fortunately, Toulmin and Goodfield (1961) noted, "the conditions for intellectual life remained good, owing to the religious tolerance of early Islam".

Within 150 years of its founding, the Islamic Empire had established its domain over a 4,000 mile arc that extended from the Atlantic coast of southern Spain across North Africa and the Middle East to the Ganges River in India. As it spread, it became heir to the intellectual traditions of many ancient civilization, including numerous manuscripts of ancient Greek science through its encounters with scattered colonies of Hellenistic scholars in Persia and elsewhere. Other scientific traditions had developed quasi-independently from the seeds of Greek science that were spread as far eastward as India during Alexander the Great's military campaigns a thousand years earlier. Those traditions also enriched the Islamic culture as it expanded its conquests.

In 7620 A.D., Baghdad was founded near the site of the ancient city of Babylon, and the new city became the cultural center of the thriving Islamic civilization. An Arabic university was established at Baghdad, and many ancient manuscripts were sent there to be translated into Arabic. Islamic science resulted from "the natural fusion of all these precious legacies" (Goldstein, 1980), and Baghdad succeeded Alexandria as the scholarly center of natural philosophy. For approximately two centuries, natural philosophers enjoyed patronage at Baghdad, and the period from 800 to 1,000 AD is recognized as the Golden Age of Islamic science. Within those centuries, the intellectual community at Baghdad had collected and assimilated nearly a thousand years of ancient natural philosophy.

By 1,000 A.D., natural philosophers at Baghdad had come to the cutting edge of science. Some, such as Avicenna (980–1037A.D.), who had conceived a dynamic, natural origin of mountain chains over long period of time, were beginning to suggest radical hypotheses. Had these been developed, they may have had a profound impact on the history of science, but "these insights were not followed up" (Toulmin and Goodfield, 1965). By this time, the political power of Islam was declining, and the disenchantment with natural philosophy that had spelled doom for science in ancient Rome began to repeat itself. The Muslim civilization's concern turned to political stability, and the atmosphere turned to one of religious intolerance. The heyday of the empire was past, and the changes eclipsed the early Islamic tradition of open inquiry. The Golden Age of Muslim science came to an end.

By 1100 A.D., the center of Islamic intellectual activity had shifted from Baghdad to the remote outposts of Southern Spain and Sicily. Science was on the run again, this time westward to the volantile border between the antagonistic Spanish Muslims and the Christians of France and Italy. In the end, the tradition of the Islamic scholar was basically one of collection, translation, and refinement of existing knowledge rather than original inquiry or theory production. The science that returned to the West in the twelfth century was, therefore, essentially a refined version of the same science that Islam had inherited five centuries earlier.

Goldstein attributed the character of Islamic science to a culturally induced disinterest in theoretical scientific pursuits. Inspired by their culture's passion for natural detail, he noted, Muslim scientists produced a profusion of concrete information based on detailed observations, but little in the way of abstract scientific conjecture. Muslim science was motivated by "the pleasurable observation of nature's diversity and the use of its bounty to the enhancement of life" (Goldstein, 1980). The Islamic culture looked on the Earth as a lovely garden, he note, and "it had little concern for establishing the mastery of mind over nature......or for proving human power through the relentless technological transformation of natural environment".

Toulmin and Goodfield attributed the Arabic lack of scientific creativity to the limited duration of intellectual freedom prior to the decline of science in Islam. However, substantial improvements were made in particular areas of science by the Muslims, they noted, notably in medicine and chemistry.

> But in astronomy and dynamics, they had time only to digest and adapt the existing traditions. They developed and greatly improved the astronomical instruments left to them by the Greeks : notably the astrolabe. ....They made fresh estimates of the size of the earth and the relative distances of the

> planets.........but made no fundamental changes in Ptolemy's methods. Certainly they never questioned the central features of his picture : at most, they tried to bring it more closely into line with the ideas of Aristotle.

In the medieval Muslim culture, Goldstein (1980) indicated, the appeal of science was primarily related to pragmatic social and commercial interests. There was little incentive to develop natural philosophy as an ideology in its own right. The medieval Arabs were a highly creative and intellectually capable society in their own right, as indicated by their brilliant mathematical achievements; but the traditional objective of Islamic science was concrete detail, and abstract theory was simply not a cultural desideratum. The medieval Muslim civilization valued science primarily as an established body of interesting and useful information about nature. Ultimately, the emphasis was on detailed treatises on nature, or ancient histories, not science. Islamic contributions were, therefore, primarily in the form of technological innovations and refinements of existing scientific knowledge.

Islam did contribute a radical new perception of science as a practical enterprise. Specific contributions included the application of existing science to practical problems such as navigation and health care. The Muslims also conceived science as a diversified body of specialized knowledge and restored to natural philosophy the early Greek notion of nature as reality, rather than a philosophical idea. The Muslim interest in ancient astronomy and physics resulted in a science-based technology of navigation and a practical union of science and commerce. Trade was central to the Arabic culture, and it was necessary for merchants' camel caravans to travel at night to avoid the devastating daylight heat of the vast deserts that characterized the Islamic empire. Ptolemy's science of astronomy, which was recognized for its accuracy, was highly valued as a means to improved night-time navigation.

Islam also developed a science of medicine and a comprehensive system of health care, including the world's first network of independently functioning hospitals. The Greeks, whose science Islam inherited, had seen illness as a natural process subject to treatment by natural means; and Islamic physicians built on that tradition. By 1100 A.D., Goldstein (1980) observed, Islam possessed a skilled medical profession employing the careful observations of symptoms and the prescription of curative agents or surgical procedures based on centuries of accumulated physiological studies and medical experience.

Islam's perfection of the Arabic numbers system was perhaps its greatest contribution. The system "was able to reduce the cosmos to a system of ten elementary symbols" (Goldstein, 1980), and quickly replaced the cumbersome and confusing number systems of the ancient Egyptian, Greek, and Roman systems. It allowed "almost perfect technical efficiency in the manipulation of numbers" (Whitehead, 1941). The development of algebra made it possible to manipulate unknown factors and to quickly demonstrate and equate complexly related, abstract quantities of virtually unlimited scope (Goldstein, 1980). Although science emerged from the medieval Islamic era much as it had entered it, the mathematics that emerged in the 12th century was drastically different from that which had characterized the ancient era.

The Arabs employed their new mathematics extensively in business and technology, but the use of the numbers system for purposes of scientific development was virtually unheard of in Islam. Even the reconciliation of Aristotelian physics and Ptolemaic astronomy had proceeded essentially non-mathematical lines. Therefore, the Muslims' developments in mathematics had little effect on the nature of the science they cherished; but the potential of their versatile new system for the scientific enterprise was demonstrated several centuries later with the development of the dynamic theories of Galileo, Newton, and others. Without the progress in Islamic mathematics during the Middle Ages, modern science would not have been possible.

For nearly a thousand years, the interest in the Greek traditions of scientific inquiry had remained dormant throughout most of Europe. Had it not been for the enthusiastic collection and translation of ancient manuscripts by the Islamic invaders, much of the scientific productivity of the ancient Greek scientists might have been lost. In addition to preserving the Greek scientific tradition and giving the world a powerful new system of mathematics, the Muslims also established an unprecedented new tradition of *applied science*. Like the ancient Babylonians and Egyptians who accumulated hundreds of years of observations upon which early Greek scientists could test their theories, Islamic scientists accumulated a tremendous additional reservoir of concrete information about nature upon which Renaissance theorists could ultimately base new concepts. For centuries, scientific inquiry had remained largely dormant, except for a brief stirring in Baghdad around 800–1000 A.D. During that brief time, theoretical inquiry into the workings of nature was on the threshold of a re-awakening; but by 1100 A.D., that interest had flickered to dormancy. Again science lay asleep, so to speak; and it would not be revived until another era and another culture.

For nearly a millennium, most of Western Europe had existed in quiescent religious resignation. Theological tradition was the prevalent authority for interpretation of human affairs, and the study of nature was generally valued "only as a source of allegories, which were used to illustrate the virtues and beauties of the spiritual life" (Toulmin and Godfield, 1961). There was simply no place for the scientific point of view in Christendom at the time. The emphasis was wholly on things spiritual; and the senses, which are essential to empirical to empirical observations of nature, were not considered reliable sources of knowledge. To question basic principles of the prevailing cosmology on the basis of sensible phenomena probably would have been considered irrational. In such a climate, it is not surprising that the appearance of the Crab Nebula supernova was not recorded by the Europeans.

> We may explain the apparent failure of the Europeans to observe and record the appearance of the Crab Nebula supernova in A.D. 1054, even though it was apparent to Chinese and American Indian observers, by noting that such an observation implies the non-immutability of the heavens, contrary to the commonly (European) accepted scriptural cosmology.

That the supernova was not recorded by the Europeans is a matter of historical fact. That it was not *observed* (assuming that Saperstein's sense of the term connotes attentive notice for purposes of learning something) illustrates the epistemological significance of cultural tradition. Many Europeans, who were geographically intermediate to the known observes, must have seen and puzzled over the supernova which was visible in daylight for a time. Medieval Christendom was committed to the authority of scripture and Christian tradition, and both indicated that the heavens were unchangeable. Probably, the spectacular supernova was not systematically observed and recorded because it was not perceived as meaningful.

Five hundred years later, when a revolutionary new world view was taking form in Western Europe, the concept of Stellar immutability was suspect and a nova that appeared in 1572 was observed as "giving fact that the heavens were alterable" (Orlich, 1964). In the emerging cosmology of the 16th century, the condition of the heavens was a major question; and observations of a nova produced meaningful scientific data. In the very different world of the 11th century, however, there was no such question that would given meaning to a supernova.

In all likelihood, the Crab Nebula supernova was viewed with much interest, but a single sensible phenomenon was not enough to shake the religious resolve of a struggling society that, centuries earlier, had denounced the natural world as illusionary. If additional occurrences had been observed, Christendom would have been challenged to question its tradition; but novae that are visible to the unaided eye are very uncommon. Today, extraneous data that cannot be accommodated by the established research tradition are generally not considered appropriate subjects for study within normal scientific communities (Kuhn, 1970). From this perspective, the intellectuals of medieval Christendom were no more and no less irresponsible than modern scientists in the dismissal of apparently insignificant data that could not be accommodated within their established cosmological tradition.

During the late Middle Ages, however, conditions in Western Europe began to change. By the 12th century, the feudal system of localized government had gradually overcome the perennial threats of invasions from the north, and the declining condition of the Muslim empire had reduced the threat from the South and East. Under the relative peace and social stability that finally prevailed, the trauma of the collapse of Rome was healed and a vibrant new culture emerged. Political expansion occurred as European armies pushed across the collapsing Islamic borders into Southern Spain and Sicily. Trade flourished, and cultural exchange generated by travels of merchants brought new ideas and new things into the West. The once isolated, passive society of Western Europe was undergoing "the first vigorous stirrings of a new cultural vitality, primarily in France" (Goldstein, 1980). Manufacturing, trade, and travel continued to increase, and a restless, searching society envisioned "new social realities that were opening tempting glimpses of the here and now, the contemporary,........more prosperous world, which was, in turn, opening up a vast prospect of the world of nature". Amidst the excitement of political expansion and prosperity, and the associated increase in leisure time, an atmosphere of enthusiasm and interest in learning developed. As the ancient Greek manuscripts fell into the hands of Westerners, and interest in ancient traditions was generated.

The new society that developed in the towns of Western Europe reflected the energy and vitality of the early Roman civilization, but it "had little in common with the defunct world of Rome, beyond ..... a thin thread of tradition" (Goldstein, 1980, p. 58). Prior to that time, interest in nature and natural philosophy had been almost obliterated in Christendom. "In rebuilding the scientific tradition after A.D.1000, therefore, men in Western Europe had in effect to start from scratch" (Toulmin and Goodfield, 1961). The rejection of the world of nature was quickly coming to an end, however, and the era of cultural flux known as the Renaissance was emerging.

In the early years of the ninth century, Charlemagne (742-814) had prodded the churches and monasteries to open "schools for the general education of boys and girls" (Durant, 1950). In the tenth century, the first cathedral school was established at Charters, France. Soon other schools were established, and these were unique in their concentration on classical studies. Up to this time, Toulmin and Goodfield (1961) observed, learning had been valued only for purposes of improving the soul; but the teachers at Charters "encouraged learning of all sorts—for its own sake". Other schools and universities encouraged similar programs, but at first most of the schools had to make do with only a few fragments of ancient literature. The teachers were "quick to take advantage of the new intellectual contacts with the Arabs", and translations of ancient manuscripts were brought to Christendom with enthusiasm akin to that with which the Arabs had collected the original Greek manuscripts centuries earlier.

It was to this receptive atmosphere that science returned, after nearly a thousand years of exile, in Europe. "After 1150, as wealth and leisure grew, and translations began to pour in from Islam, the mind of Western Europe was aroused from its torpor, curiosity flared into eagerness" (Durant, 1950). By the early 1300s, "all the important doctrines of antiquity were known" (Toulmin and Goodfield, 1961). However, the interest in science was more or less a fad, according to Goldstein (1980): "The study of nature was an intellectual delight, not necessarily a stern and specialized academic pursuit". As was the case in ancient Greece, science was more or less an elite intellectual activity indulged in by a few persistent persons whose social position provided the leisure time and learning for the pursuit of such ideas. Schooling was very limited for most people, and science was still not recognized as an important part of their past, present, or future. It would be another 300 years before a new scientific tradition would be established and the socio-cultural benefits of the Islamic concept of applied science would be realized. With the cultural and social changes that opened the door to that new tradition would also come an unprecedented perception of a social utility of scientific inquiry and an equally unprecedented concept of public science education.

Science did not suddenly explode upon the scene in the Renaissance no did it lead the cultural flux of the era. Rather, "the Renaissance gave its soul to art, leaving a little for literature, less for philosophy, least for science" (Durant, 1953). Science was neither widely known nor recognized as an important part of society's past, present, or future. This soon changed, however; and the history of modern science became inextricably interwoven with the history of Western civilization.

During the early years of the Renaissance, the scientific traditions of the ancient Greeks and medieval Islamics were viewed with increasing interest throughout Europe. Eventually the interest turned to action as an increasingly restless European civilization looked beyond the seclusion of the Middle Ages toward a bigger and more hospitable world. Intrigued by the ancient Greek concept of an Earth surrounded by a navigable ocean sphere, for example and inspired by Islam's successful use of Ptolemy's astronomy for desert navigation, and encouraged by the invention of the magnetic compass, a few daring European sailors ventured into the unknown seas. Their safe return and fantastic stories of adventure and treasure inspired others; and by A.D. 1522, the Americas had been discovered and the Earth had been circumnavigated.

The wonders of geographic discovery overwhelmed the European world. Once the contributions of Greek and Hellenistic science to these discoveries were realized, there was a surge of public interest in natural philosophy. By the middle of the 17th century, but still a half century before Isaac Newton formulated the basic principles of modern science, the interest had turned to fervor. Science, still generally known as "natural philosophy", was enthusiastically perceived as the source of "Utopia and the savior of mankind" (Durant and Durant, 1963). Out of the Renaissance came an unprecedented concept of science as having significant social relevance, and with it a perceived need for a government-supported program of science education for all citizens. Preceding the full realization of these ideals, however, there were major reinterpretations of both the nature and purposes of history and science.

By the early 1600s, Francis Bacon (1561–1626) and his peers predicted that science would produce great practical benefits by making society the masters of nature (Durant and Durant, 1961). This was an unprecedented concept—the Islamics had advocated a social utility of existing science information, but neither they nor their Greek predecessors advocated the mastery of nature for human benefit—and it was a highly questionable prediction, considering the world-view that prevailed at the time. Nevertheless, Western society was soon enthralled with the prospects of employing the intellect to take control of nature for purposes of secular human power and social benefit.

That goal was not immediately achieved, however, for a reason that, for many people, rendered it an essentially moot objective. The Renaissance society, although characterized as restless and searching, was slow to change. For more than a thousand years, religious tradition had held that human destiny was fixed between relatively recent creation and non-too-distant destruction of the world. Humanity, according to Christian tradition, had been divinely created in a perfect state and placed in a perfect garden. Soon, however, the human creature demonstrated an imperfect character and was expelled to a less hospital environment. In addition, human imperfection was believed to have infected nature itself (Toulmin and Goodfield, 1965). Humanity and the nature it touched were perceived as degenerating toward a terminal condition, and history was a providential revelation of that decline. Even the great mechanistic genius of Leonardo da Vinci (1452-1519) was eclipsed by the specter of inevitable doom as society looked back upon ancient civilizations and intellectual accomplishments that supposedly could never be equaled, and a deep sense of pessimism settled over the European world.

In his *History of the World* (1602), Sir Walter Raleigh (1552?-1618) reflected the traditional historians' point of view when he calculated that the end of the world would come around 1968. Many, however, saw the end as much more imminent; and some believed that the novel ideas of scientists such as Copernicus (1473-1543), Galileo (1564-1642), and Kepler (1571-1630) were a contributing factor. But most Renaissance thinkers did not attribute such power to the human intellect. They felt that those strange ideas were a symbol, rather than a cause, of the breakdown of the natural order of things (Santillana, 1956).

The World was breaking down, they believed; and the novel things that Galileo and others reported were taken as evidence of its dying spasms. Whereas the Crab Nebula had been dismissed as meaningless five centuries earlier, Tyco Brahe's (1546-1601) sixteenth century observations of a comet and nova were seen as evidence that the degeneration had spread into the heavens. Seeing no hope of a future for humanity, a despondent civilization settled in to contemplate its end on the eve of the Scientific Revolution. History was valued for whatever moral instruction it could provide to a society that was preoccupied with preparing for a spiritual afterlife.

Fortunately, there was a minority point of view regarding history and the destiny of humanity. For example, the English statesman Francis Bacon contended that history should be viewed in terms of cultural development, not degeneration. He had served for 19 years in the British Parliament, and his ideas grew out of a statesman's sincere concern for the social welfare. Francis Bacon viewed books as little "boats with precious cargos launched on the great sea of time" (Eiseley, 1973) and he searched those cargos for insight into the human condition. From that search, Bacon concluded that the past should not be looked upon as perfection nor the future as lost.

Antiquity represented the naive beginning rather than the pinnacle of civilization, he boldly declared; and history should be considered a chronicle of a maturing civilization from which even further growth might be patterned.

> So Bacon became one of the first true modern historians ....
> he was prepared to treat the men and events of his own age as significant in their own right. If anything, he argued, the men of modern times had built on the achievements of the ancients and so surpassed them.

The idea of an inevitable end of the world persisted, however, until the 18th century concept of geological time finally shattered the sacred 6,000 years time table. So for Bacon and his 17th-century colleagues, the end still loomed near. But while awaiting the inevitable, they saw no reason why society should not attempt to make those last years as comfortable as possible.

A comfortable environment was an intrinsically worthy goal, Bacon concluded, and society was justified in taking control of nature to achieve it. Bacon's radical new point of view, which was published in *The advancement of Learning* around in 1605, broke completely with Western tradition regarding both the criteria of human progress and the meaning of history. Traditionally, human progress had been perceived in transcendental terms of personal struggle and sacrifice for the edification of the soul. But he conceived it in terms of secular human welfare—and in doing so laid the philosophical ground work for the modern concept of applied science.

Likewise, history had been interpreted as depicting a fixed human destiny. Bacon, however, saw it as basis for systematic study of human options—and in doing so laid the philosophical ground-work for the modern concept of history. All types of societies and governments hand flourished and faltered in the past, he observed; and a proper study of history should reveal the causes of their ups and downs. From such a study, he concluded, a plan for a better civilization could be built. That redefinition of history justifies his acclaim as "The Man Who Saw Through Time" (Eiseley, 1973).

Bacon's radical ideal of a social utility of history constituted a revolution in the concept of the nature and meaning of history akin, in scope and philosophical significance, to the new ideas of science that characterized the Scientific Revolution. Renaissance society's interest in the Baconian notion that it could employ history to build a better civilization precipitated a new cultural perception of the value of the study of human events that, for lack of a better term, deserves distinction as *The Historical Revolution*.

On the basis of his concept of the meaning of history, Francis Bacon searched the histories of past and present civilizations for those factors that had most affected society's cultural development and strength. Citing benefits of mechanical inventions such as the compass, printing press, and gunpowder, he concluded that technological development showed the greatest potential for building a strong, new world. The modern concept of applied science was finally formalized when he declared that science is the tool with which civilization may achieve the end of technological progress.

So for Francis Bacon, science was more than the natural history appreciated by the ancient Mesopotamians or the practical body of knowledge cherished by the medieval Muslims. It was more than the intellectual system the ancient Greeks valued for understanding their place in nature, and it was more than a source of insight into the divine plan for the World as conceived by medieval Christendom. It was also a *work* that could be done to change the world for the better. "The true and lawful goal of the sciences," Bacon wrote, "is none other than this: that human life be endowed with new powers and discoveries". He took as his life's goal the task of prescribing a methodology through which society pursue that end.

Because of Aristotle's heavy dependence on deductive logic, Bacon rejected the Aristotelian tradition of science. He proposed an alternative based on inductive generalization from experience (Salmon, 1967). In the *Navum Organum* (published in 1620) and *The New Atlantis* (1624), he described a new philosophy of science that, he confidently predicted, would answer all important scientific questions. His system was based on an inductive methodology, however, that would severely tax—if not overwhelm—today's most advanced data processing capabilities. Ironically, Durant and Durant (1961) noted, Bacon also discounted the works of his contemporary, Galileo. He recognized the advantages of Galileo's use of scientific hypotheses as guides for further observation, but was concerned that some hypothetical conditions might appear so obvious that they, like Aristotle's logic, would cause observers to disregard contrary evidence.

In the end, Bacon had an accurate vision of the future of science, but not its development. He foresaw the modern association of science and technology and the benefits of empiricism, for example, but remained committed to Ptolemy's geocentric concept of the universe. Ultimately, many of his ideas were dismissed as naive. Furthermore, in 1621 Bacon was impeached and banned from public service for accepting gratuities from persons appealing to his office. This indiscretion, and his adherence to the Ptolemaic cosmos (which was not an unreasonable choice at the time, considering the scientific evidence that was available), discredited his works in future years.

Nevertheless, Bacon made several very important contributions to the future development of science. Among the greatest was his optimistic reinterpretation of the nature of history. His new concept of the past appealed to the restless secularism that had been building in Western civilization since the late Middle Ages, and it inspired a social confidence that finally displaced the pessimism that had prevailed in Europe since the collapse of the Roman Empire. This in turn generated a social receptivity to his then-radical ideas of the purposeful application of science to the problems of building a better civilization. The revolutionary concept of the nature and meaning of history also enabled the later development of science. For example, Bacon's non-providential basis of history is inherent in both the mechanistic cosmic systems that characterize Newtonian science and the speciational concepts that undergird Darwin's evolutionary theory of biological development.

Becon's enthusiasm for the social utility of science culminated in what may be his greatest contribution—the concept of science education. In *The Advancement of Learning*, published in 1605, he proposed an elaborate plan for the systematic development and dissemination of scientific knowledge. Many of his suggestions are remarkably appropriate nearly four centuries later. For example :

> He calls for the multiplication and support of colleges, libraries, laboratories, biological gardens, museums of science and industry; for the better payment of teachers and researchers; for ampler funds to finance scientific experiments.

In *The New Atlantis*, Bacon advocated an intimate union of science and government to insure the resources needed for technological advancement. He also proposed the classification and application of the sciences to appropriate fields of research. Mass education of scientists and technologists was proposed to staff a large number of specialized, problem-solving laboratories. Each laboratory, much as Thomas Edison's did two and a half centuries later, would produce inventions on a wholesale basis—with each invention scientifically fitted to the fulfillment of human need. This called for a new cultural institution : science education. With an effective program of public science education, Bacon believed, any society could produce many great scientists and advance scientific development. An occasional genius might still come along, he admitted, but the progress of science would no longer be dependent on the sporadic appearance of exceptional individuals such as Aristotle.

It is significant that, from the outset, Bacon deemed the education of all citizens to be essential to the appropriate development of science. He saw science as a public teachable entity with which society could produce a better world; but he clearly declared that it was no panacea. The technological arts may promote as well as prevent human misery, he warned; and scientific development and the new technology it may produce could, therefore, be either a boon or bane, depending upon the nature of its use or abuse.

The society that would exploit science, he believed, must accept responsibility for its application and accommodate its affect. Perhaps troubled by his own laxity in a position of power, he emphasized that a public program of liberal education, including literature and philosophy, was necessary to insure wise public judgement in the support of scientific activity. The advancement of science alone was not the key to a better future; rather, it must be accompanied by an equally significant advancement of human character if society is to cope with the social and cultural change produced by scientific and technological development.

On that basis, Bacon conceived three distinct threats to a successful relationship of science and society: an inadequate supply of competent scientists; a lack of public understanding and support of science; and avaricious leadership. The first threat could be handled by building sound programs for recruiting and training scientists and technologists. The second threat could be lessened by including science as a basic competent of an extensive program of public education. The third could be reduced by placing equal emphasis on studies that would teach essential human values and social ideals as well as science.

Tremendous power will accrue to the society that exploits the potential of applied science, Bacon declared; and an educated citizenry will be essential to insure the reasoned direction of that power. It is, therefore, essential that science and education be advanced together if society is to maintain the potential for a better life through science and technology. In other words, he believed, the benefits of science are dependent upon an educated society.

Bacon, like Galileo, lived in the dawn of modern science; and both were world-shakers in their won right. As a statesman, Bacon dared to look beyond historical tradition in search of a better destiny for civilization. As a natural philosopher, Galileo dared to look beyond scientific tradition for new insight into the nature of things. Had there been Bacon alone, the 17th-century surge of scientific curiosity might have bogged down under the burden of unmanageable methodology and inadequate cosmic theory. But there was Galileo, whose telescopic observations exposed the heavens to detailed scrutiny and whose techniques of experimentation earned him acclaim as *The Inventor of Experimental Science.*

Had there been Galileo alone, his ideas might have languished amidst an apathetic society awaiting the end of the physical world. But there was Bacon, whose radical interpretation of the meaning of history swung society's attention toward visions of a better life—and whose enthusiasm for science as the key to that better life helped to fan the flicker of scientific curiosity into a bonfire of interest. Having justified the potential social value of science, Bacon found himself challenged with the problem of communicating science to the society. He turned with characteristic zeal to the development of a system of public education that would prepare a citizenry with a balanced, interdisciplinary background appropriate for the equitable development and deployment of science. Finally, his eloquent advocacy of general public participation in the scientific enterprise elevated the teaching of science to the level of social necessity; and this justifies his designation as *The Inventor of Science Education.*

In the centuries since Francis Bacon proposed his revolutionary ideas about the role of science in society, history has justified both his enthusiasm and caution. Science and technology have produced benefits beyond his greatest dreams, and both have become essential components of modern culture. There have also been problems reminiscent of Bacon's gravest concerns about the dangers of scientific development outpacing society's ability to cope with change. Practical problems include environmental pollution and the threat of nuclear catstrophe. Cultural issues include changing employment patterns and the influence of science on traditional human values.

Some people have blamed scientific and technological development for our problems, Bybee (1979) noted while others have seen science and technology as the solution to our problems. "Both positions," he declared, "are partially correct and partially wrong."

> It is not science and technology per se that cause the problems; rather, it is human ideas and values about scientific development and technological application that have both contributed to our progress and potential collapse.

Bybee's comments reflected Bacon's warning that scientific development must be accompanied by effective public education to produce a scientifically enlightened citizenry. Recognition of the importance of such a populace for the well-being of both science and society has elevated science education to the level of a national priority in the United States of America.

Science education did not begin to emerge as a major concern in this country until the last half of the 19th century, nearly two and a half centuries after Bacon. By that time science and technology had become the dominant cultural forces Bacon had envisioned, but science education had not kept pace. Science was receiving increasing attention as a curricular component, but the value of science education was perceived in a variety of ways. A diversity of special interest groups ranging from agricultural and vocational advocates, moral reformers, temperance groups, humane societies, and health groups "demanded that their concerns be incorporated into science education" (Petersom et al.,m 1984). As a result, the value of science education was perceived in a variety of ways.

Rapid technological change in the late 1800s, for example, created a demand for a more utilitarian emphasis on science per se. This resulted in the *elementary science movement,* which emphasized the contributions of scientific theories to technology and was promoted as a means to fulfilling "the need for skilled labor in the rapidly developing technology" (Underhill, 1941). On the other hand, advocates of *object teaching*, which was popular from about 1860 to the 1880s, saw science largely as a source of material for use in mental-discipline exercises. Widespread concern for the emotional development of children in the early years of elementary education contributed to development of a third program called *nature study*, which, among other things, was promoted as developing children's aesthetic and emotional values. Rivalry between the advocates of the elementary science and nature study movements was often intense from the 1890s into the early years of the twentieth century. However, neither of the programs achieved its ideals, Underhill concluded, because of "a broad lack of knowledge of science on the part of the teacher".

The Industrial Revolution was in full swing by 1900, and the United States had become a major industrial power. Technological developments over the previous half century produced a new life-style of unprecedented material comfort and convenience. The new life-styles of unprecedented material comfort and convenience. The new life-style was accompanied by a marked change in employment patterns, and technical education became increasingly important for competition in the job market. Still, science education was far from a major social force.

World War I (1914–1918) was among the more influential factors that contributed to an increased emphasis on science as a major curricular objective. The United States had emerged from the conflict as an acknowledged world power, and technological capability had played a significant role in the victory. The nation came to realize that scientific development could be a critical factor in national defense.

Little more than a quarter-century later, in 1945, the nation emerged from World War II as an undisputed superpower and sole possessor of the secret of nuclear energy. The United States was a new wonderland of science; and great scientists migrated to the U.S. with enthusiasm akin to that of the natural philosophers who flocked to ancient Alexandria and medieval Baghdad. A feeling of national pride and security in the power of science prevailed, and no problem seemed too big nor any goal too remote for the resources of modern science and technology.

In 1949, however, just four years into the Atomic Age, Soviet Russia also laid claim to the secret of nuclear power. In 1952, the U.S. reasserted its technological supremacy with the detonation of a hydrogen bomb, but just a year later this time, the Soviets detonated a hydrogen bomb. This created concern among the nation's political and scientific communities; but to the average American citizen, the Soviets were just following the leader. The

United States was still the undisputed world leader in science and technology, and most Americans believed it was just a matter of time until another great scientific feat would make that quite clear.

The confidence seemed justified. American technology had produced the first supersonic flight in 1947; and by the early 1950s, engineers were designing a person-carrying spacecraft. In 1955, the federal government "published a detailed description of the rockets that would be used to launch a small satellite in late 1957 or early 1958" (Wolfe, 1979). These developments generated increased interest in science education; and from 1945 to 1955, "virtually all..... (secondary students were) exposed to at least two years of general science" (Lacey, 1966). From this, it would appear that all was well with science education in the United States—but this was not the case.

Student testing during World War II had revealed weaknesses in the areas of science and mathematics (Lacey, 1966). In response, many studies on the condition of science education were conducted over the next decade. One such study, the "Bush Report" (*Science, the Endless Frontier*, which was published in 1945), had far-reaching implications for science education. The United States had developed an extensive scientific enterprise in World War II, and President Roosevelt asked Vannever Bush to examine ways that the power of science might be redirected to peace-time pursuits. The Bush Report "led to the establishment of the National Science Foundation in 1950 and ......(highlighted) the need to improve science instruction at all levels of education" (Buccino, 1983).

The Bush Report prompted another study by the American Association for the Advancement of Science (AAAS) in 1946. That study attributed the condition of science education to three major problems—all anticipated by Francis Bacon's concern for the adequate support of science education:

> The American public ....fails to pay its teachers decently, ... colleges and universities........failed to prepare prospective teachers for the kind of teaching they should do ....(and) the high school curriculum needs a thoroughgoing reorganization.

Reaction to the Bush Report and the AAAS study precipitated action. In 1953, the NSF implemented a series of programs to improve science education. In 1954, the National Science Teachers Association (NSTA) initiated a program to recognize and award outstanding teachers (Lacey, 1966). Science education had clearly become a matter of national policy, and a determined movement for reform was gathering momentum.

Then something happened that riveted the nation's attention to the issue of science education. In October, 1957, the Soviet Union placed the world's first artificial satellite in orbit around the Earth. The United states' cherished position of superiority in science and technology was lost as Sputnik beeped overhead, and pressure for reform in science education suddenly intensified to the proportions of a revolution. Whatever the scientific and technological significance of Sputnik, its social and political impact was galvanizing. "The fact that the Soviets had the rocket power to launch Sputnik meant that they now also had the capacity to deliver the bomb on an intercontinental ballistic missile" (Wolfe, 1979).

Being second did not come easy to a young civilization accustomed to being first. The nation's ego had been badly bruised and its confidence severely shaken by Sputnik, and the desire to catch up became an obsession. Many who remember those frantic days blush at the recall of the nation's first entries into the space race. Effort after effort to launch a satellite—all televised for the world to see—ended in flaming failure. It was a time of national humiliation and uncertainty, and the crisis rhetoric that characterized the era magnified the public concern. The Soviets continued to dominate in space as they put the first human in orbit. The production of the scientists and engineers needed to catch up with the Soviets became an immediate national priority. With a critical but hopeful eye, a desperate nation turned its attention—and its money—to the support of science education.

The NSF had declared a need for reforms in science education, and a reform movement had started in the schools. Soon all eyes were on the schools, and it was there that the blame was laid and the hope was placed. Billions of dollars were devoted to science education—often without question (Yager, 1981), and a new direction in science education soon emerged.

Previously, science education was valued primarily for student—centered purposes such a social and vocational competence. But the curricular reformers of the early 1960s generally adopted Bruner's subject-centered model of education, which placed primary emphasis on "the underlying principles that give structure to ......(a science) subject" (Bruner, 1960). Previously, most school science text books had been written by educators; but by the late 1950s, the central involvement of scientists was considered essential to he development of science curricula (Butts, 1982). A new series of NSF-funded programs was developed along that line; and many are commonly known by the acronyms of their titles, such as BSCS (Biological Science Curriculum Study), SCIS (Science Curriculum Improvement Study), ESS (Elementary Science Study), and SAPA (Science—A Process Approach). Such studies were taken up in other countries also.

By 1962, a subject-centered emphasis clearly prevailed, and NSTA adopted the position that "science proper........should be the primary goal of scientific education" (NSTA, 1962) "The (new) curriculum reflected the discipline of the scientist," Butts (1982) observed,"and not the social problems, life, skills, or contextual, environmental concerns" of earlier science education.

Hundreds of new educational programs were launched in the late 1950s and early 1960s. But some were based on convincing presuppositions that, in retrospect, lacked adequate philosophical justification; and others lacked adequate planning and organization. Four years after Sputnik, the executive director of the NSTA expressed a growing concern :

> All of us are caught up in "the pursuit of excellence," but all too often, the pursuit becomes a mad rush to "do something, even though we are not sure it is right." Reasons for this, perhaps, are that we seldom take time to think and spell out what is meant by excellence.

Nevertheless, interest and enthusiasm for science education were high, and students entering college soon appeared to be better prepared in science (Lacey, 1966). Furthermore, Butts (1982) noted, "by 1970 the goal of a man on the moon was achieved, and internationally our position as 'number one' in science was recaptured" (p. 1669). In many ways it appeared that the 1960s had ushered in a Golden Age for science education in the United States. Several events occurred in the 1960s and 1970s, however, that led to a reorientation of national priorities.

Chief among the events leading to a reorientation of national educational priorities was the struggle for civil rights and human equality in the 1960s and 1970s.

> Just as Sputnik has provided the visible symbol to justify federal support for the improvement of science education, the assassinations of John F. Kennedy, Martin Luther King, and Robert Kennedy provided the visible justification for allocating billions of dollars toward nationally supported economic and educational equity programs. Thus, without fanfare, the greatest nationally supported reformation in science education was gradually and completely over-shadowed by the human rights movement.

Twice within a decade, the United States had been shocked to the core with the reality of vulnerability. The first shock, Sputnik, represented a clearly identified threat from the outside. The second shock, the assassinations of the nation's president and leading proponents of civil rights and human equality, represented a less clearly defined threat from within. The first threat had focused the American public's attention on the importance of the advancement of science, and the nation responded with a wholehearted commitment of resources. The second threat turned the nation's attention toward the importance of the advancement of human character, and the country responded with an equally wholehearted commitment.

Education was again conceived as the key and society turned once more to its schools for deliverance. This time, as before, there was extensive pressure for curricular change. This time, as before, there was much impulsive action, sometimes without sufficient planning or philosophical justification. Given the country's continuing interest in science for the space race and national defense, it is conceivable that both science education and educational equity would have shared positions of top priority. But there were other influencing factors.

By the late 1960s, Vietnam War had generated serious public concern regarding the efficacy of advanced military technology in the current arena of international politics. Growing public awareness of such problems as environmental pollution, hazardous waste management, and industrial nuclear accidents raised additional questions about the nation's investment in science and technology. Rapid scientific and technological development also contributed to changing employment patterns. The resulting social stress led some to believe that science caused too much change too fast and that it was insensitive to human needs and values (Etzioni and Nunn, 1974).

Public confidence in science began to decline by the mid 1960s. By the end of the decade, the United States had succeeded in the spectacular and much publicized goal of putting a human on the moon, but even this did not stay the changing public attitude toward science. As the world watched the first human footsteps on the moon, most people were aware of some of the spectacular contributions of science as well some of its undesirable side-effects; but there was little general understanding of either the actual or desirable relationship of science to society. Similarly, there was little public understanding of the nature and purposes of science, or the distinction between science, technology, and engineering. By the 1980s, it was painfully clear that the nation's science education efforts had not kept pace with its scientific and technological development. Educators began to use the term "crisis" to describe the condition of science education in the United States.

Three-and-a-half centuries earlier, Francis Bacon had predicted the need for effective science education to help society accommodate the tremendous change that applied science would produce. Furthermore, he saw the direction of applied science as the responsibility of all the people—not just the scientific community, government agencies, or any other subset of society. Otherwise, the scientific enterprise might perish for lack of public trust and support. Or perhaps even more ominous, the great power of science and technology might be inequitably or irresponsibly deployed to the detriment of civilization. By the mid-1960s, and again in the 1980s, the wisdom of his prediction was confirmed by the declining public attitude toward science in this country; but the problem had been clearly recognized several decades earlier.

In 1934, John Dewey unequivocally declared that the social impact of science requires science education for the masses as well as for would-be scientists. Applied science has clearly produced many benefits for everyone, but it has also created bewildering social problems. To prevent further bewilderment, he prescribed an integrated curricular approach to keep other social institutions from lagging behind science in a rapidly changing world.

In 1947, J. B. Conant pointed out that science-related policy issues must deal with highly technical, scientific considerations. Like Bacon, he concluded that it is very important that those in positions of authority and responsibility, and especially those whose attitudes and actions may influence others, have a basic understanding of science.

However, Conant concluded, it is an oversimplification to assume that the solution to this problem is greater dissemination of factual scientific knowledge among non-scientists. The research scientist approaches problems from a particular point of view, he explained, so information that may be meaningful to a scientist may be quite bewildering to those having no research background with which to interpret it. Therefore, he proposed that the average student would be better served by historical case studies of the basic purposes and methods of science.

These ideas had generated considerable interest in curricular reform by the early 1950s; but in the reforms that followed the Sputnik era, neither Dewey's interdisciplinary ideas nor Conant's historical approach prevailed. The emphasis had suddenly shifted to the production of technical personnel to counter the Soviet threat and a discipline-specific, subject-centered approach was generally accepted as appropriate to that goal. However, the need for a scientifically competent society was neither ignored not forgotten by the science education community. Many phrases were coined to express the science background needed by the average citizen, and "*scientific literacy* (was) the term most frequently used" (Agin, 1974).

"*Scientific literacy*" had a convincing and appealing ring of legitimacy, and it was an immediately popular topic. Unfortunately, Miller (1983) indicated, use of the term became widespread long before a clear concept of its meaning was developed. From the start, science teachers were generally convinced that scientific literacy should be an educational priority; but by the mid-1960s, the futility of attempting to develop a curriculum around an inadequately defined concept had become a prominent topic (Pella, et al., 1966). On the one hand, some educators began to suspect that scientific literacy may be an unrealistic curricular goal for science education. On the other hand, scientific illiteracy was not an acceptable option.

Klopfer (1969) echoed a prevalent concern. "For every man and woman who hopes to function effectively as a citizen of society in the twentieth century, literacy in science is an essential requirement". On that basis, he declared that science education has two main purposes : requisite science training for those few students preparing for careers in science and technology; and training that will contribute to the scientific literacy of all students.

As 1970 approached, the science education community became increasingly concerned that it was not accomplishing that important second purpose. The reforms of the 1950s and 1960s had provided the sorely needed advancement of science, but the nation still lacked a citizenry that could understand and accommodate applied science. "Science and technology have come close to providing us the world mankind has been seeking for thousands of years," Hurd (1970) wrote; "however, we have not been successful in teaching man how to live successfully in this new world".

Over the thousands of years alluded to by Hurd, humanity had interpreted the "good life" in a number of ways ranging from the intellectual independence of ancient Greece to the materialism of the Roman Empire to the spiritual self-denial of the Middle Ages. Over those same years, humanity sought better living from many means, including mythology, mysticism, magic, and a multitude of religious and political systems—and recently, applied science. The latter had produced the greatest promise of a good life for humanity in modern times.

All this came to a head for the United States in the science education issues that have characterized the era from the 1960s through the 1980s. Now that American society had brought the long-sought better world closer through the power of applied science, it was faced with the problem of educating itself to accommodate and maintain that new world—or risk losing it as more and more people have second thoughts about the benefits and risks of science and technology.

Some educators and scientist expressed alarm at the relative lack of public concern over the problem outside the scientific and educational communities. The explosion of scientific knowledge has outstripped the public's ability to assimilate it, T.P. Evans (1970) concluded, and "as a result, the average citizen has disassociated himself intellectually from science." This attitude, he lamented, is a deterrent to scientific literacy that, unless overcome, will prevent the realization of that goal.

Beginning in the 1960s, however, several major public policy issues had emerged, however, that eventually helped to sensitize other groups to the immediate threat of scientific illiteracy. Many environmentalists and conservationists became alarmed that the general public lacked the basic scientific knowledge needed to understand policy debates about pollution. Government and business leaders became concerned that important projects might be stymied by unfounded public fear of possible deleterious side effects of science and technology. There was also increasing concern that serious problems might result from the lack of sufficient science backgrounds among key decision-makers involved in science-related programs or activities in government, business and industry.

Though still undefined in meaningful educational terms, "scientific literacy was suddenly catapulted to the status of major national issue. pressure for curricular change multiplied. Some educators called for drastic reforms to shift the curricular focus from science-centered to a student-centered emphasis. Evans (1970), for example, suggested avoiding the specialized language of the scientist so science could be "presented to the general public in terms it can understand." In an effort to clarify the issue, NSTA conducted a survey of science educators and convened several conferences to develop a position statement in the goals of science education in the 1970s. That statement, released in July 1971, established the long-standing consensus that "the major goal of science education is to develop scientifically literate and personally concerned individuals with a high competency of rational thought and action" (NSTA, 1971).

By the late 1980s, there was general concern that major reforms were needed in science education. The tremendous outpouring of energy in the 1960s had apparently been futile—an exercise devoid of philosophical direction. The literature of the 1970s echoed the struggles and confusion of the 1960s as writers continued to ask "what is meant by the term 'scientific literacy' ?" (N. Smith, 1974). Brovey (1980) declared that the current practices in science education were producing a nation of scientifically *aware* but scientifically *illiterate* people. Surveys commissioned by NSF during the late 1970s indicated that less than five percent of citizens outside the scientifically involved community could be classified as scientifically literate (Miller, 1983). Hazen and Trefil (1991) challenge the nation that general scientific literacy prevailed even in the scientific community: "Indeed, it has been our experience that working scientists are often illiterate outside their own field of professional expertise".

There was intense concern over the condition of science education in the 1950s, and it preceded a period of major reform. Again in the 1980s, a strong movement for reform has emerged. Although the science education profession still lacks a clear, philosophically justified definition of its boldly acclaimed goal, "scientific literacy," the struggles of the past three decades have not been fruitless. The profession now has a clear concept of its basic purpose— the dual purpose advocated by Francis Bacon three-and-a-half centuries ago: Training the specialized personnel needed to maintain the current scientific enterprise, and educating the scientifically informed public that must accommodate and direct the application of science and technology to the equitable resolution of society's problems.

The means to accomplish the first dimension of that purpose can be built upon the successful practices of the past two or three decades. The means to the second dimension, however, constitute the supreme challenge to science educators. Programs such as AAAS's Project 2061 (Rutherford and Ahlgren, 1990) and the National Science Teachers Association's (1990) project, Scope, Sequence, and Coordination of Secondary Science, have implemented field projects to assess options for radical curricular reforms. And the results of those and other studies are anxiously awaited by a concerned public that is acutely aware of the importance of the issues involved.

> By most criteria, science education is not preparing students for their role as citizens who must make informed and responsible decisions about science-related social problems during the next decades. Such problems cannot simply be turned over to scientific "aristocrats," consumer advocates, or corporate enterprises. The democratic process requires public participation, and it is assumed that the public is informed and literate.

More than 350 years earlier, in the dawn of the era of modern science, Francis Bacon had expressed similar concern about the importance of citizen participation in the direction of a nation's scientific enterprise. The history of the relation of science, technology, and society in the United States over the past 150 years further justifies Bacon's contention that a scientifically educated citizenry is an essential counterpart of scientific and technological development. The means to achieve this must be a fundamental research objective of science education, and further study of Bacon's prophetic vision of the role of science and education in a technologically advanced culture is clearly indicated as a source of insight into appropriate goals and objectives for science education in the 1990s and beyond.

The importance of a sound scientific education for the young generations is recognized by science educators of both technologically advanced societies and developing ones. The recognition of this importance is not, however, consistent with what we know about classroom practices in the natural sciences. These sciences are taught divorced from the lives of students, the problems of the surrounding community, the global implications they may have, etc..

The presentation of the natural science is, in general, text book bound, aimed at the memorization of vocabulary and the algorithmic resolution of quantitative problems. The student side of the picture is constituted by young persons that can, at best, parrot definitions, solve numerical problems, but have little understanding of ideas, very little notion of the applications of these sciences and even less critical awareness of their role in causing and/or solving societal problems. (Driver et al. 1985; Osborne & Freyberg 1985; Gallagher 1989, 1990).

We all know that the problems of science education are complex, recurrent, and difficult to solve. They have pedagogical, social, historical, and political dimensions not always clear cut and easily addressable. This should caution us about putting too much hope on solving those problems by a pedagogical path. On the other hand, pedagogical dimensions are usually within reach of science educators and may serve as an entry point into the path that may lead if not to solution at least to alleviation.

One of the solutions that has been advocated for the problems of science education is teaching for understanding. Teachers and students should engage in a set of practices whose aim and result is the understanding of the natural sciences. The purpose of this paper is to illuminate some possible ways of conceiving what it means to understand the natural sciences.

The aim of science education is conceived, in this paper, as the construction of "understanding of the natural sciences." The statement immediately raises two questions : What are viable meanings for the expression "understanding of the natural sciences"? How can we pursue it?

In general we can say that we understand something when we know what that something means. The connection of understanding and meaning is now almost traditional in the philosophy of the human sciences since the analysis of Dilthey (1990) at the turn of the century. A viable theory of understanding is then connected with a theory of meaning: Understanding the natural sciences is, therefore, understanding their meaning. What could be a viable meaning for the expression "the meaning of the natural sciences"?

Alan Bishop (1985) speaking about mathematical meaning says that making mathematical meaning for an expression, idea, concept is connecting that idea, concept etc. to other ideas in mathematics, to other ideas in fields of knowledge other than mathematics and to everyday uses of those ideas. We can use this definition as a strafing point if we think of ideas in the natural sciences instead of mathematical ideas. The definition above has important advantages but still considers meaning from the point of view of ideas, concepts, etc. what we can call, for lack of a better term, the contents of the mind. Undeniably the natural sciences are ideas, concepts, theories, explanations, facts, etc.. They are also practices, social relations, modes of discourse, and historical ways of evolving characteristic of specific communities of thought and action: Whenever were are reducing the natural sciences to ideas, concepts, etc. that are one of their products we are forgetting two things. One is that the constitution and maintenance of the scientific communities are not only producers but also products of the natural sciences. The other is that the ideas, concepts, that are produced by the natural sciences when divorced from the practices and communities where from they were produced and that are part of their meaning makes them unintelligible. Understanding the natural sciences in understanding them as a form of life with all that is part of that form of life.

Forms of life are embodied in complexes of practices, actions, and beliefs. Understanding the natural sciences is engaging in the practices that will render the form of life that the natural sciences are, intelligible. Intelligible means here no more and no less that possible of being understood and talked about in some meaningful ways. Intelligible does not mean here transparent or fully describable. The totality of any form of life will always escape us in some way.

The practices of understanding the natural sciences are certainly related to the practices of making those sciences. They are not necessarily the same nor simple transpositions into school or other contexts.

According to Wittgenstein's *Philosophical Investigations* the meaning of a word is its use in the language.

> For a large class of cases—though not for all—in which we employ the word "meaning" it can be defined thus: The meaning of a word is its use in the language.

We can extend this notion by saying that understanding an idea, a concept, an expression, means then, using it appropriately in the language (be it spoken or written). Any language evolves within a community of users. Appropriate and inappropriate uses have always to be referred to the proper community and the proper context. Wittgenstein seemed to hint at this when he wrote that "to imagine a language is to imagine a form of life." In the case of the natural sciences, students and teachers understand a concept, idea or what not, when they are able to use it correctly in the discourse. Correctly here means no more and no less than acceptable to the members of the community.

The process of coming to understand is not linearly sequential but more of a circular nature. We understand a concept or idea in so far as we use it appropriately in the language. We come to understand it correctly as we use it appropriately in the language. Using, being corrected, correcting others, and being able to anticipate the correction of others are not only criteria for understanding but also the very process by which understanding as use is constructed. Wittgenstein, in the *Philosophical Investigations* puts it very clear when he says :

> Let the use of words teach you their meaning. Similarly one can often say in mathematics : let the proof teach you what was being proved.

Putting it more clearly, we do not understand and then use but we understand as we use and we use as we come to understand. The process of constructing understanding is thus, not only circular but also endless.

The use of words expressions and concepts does not make sense unless it is bound to a community of discourse. There is no way of correctly using the words, concepts or whatever in an appropriate way unless we understand the form of life they embody and form which they spring. The reciprocal is true, we cannot understand a form of life if we do not understand the language that express it. One again we are immersed in the productive circularity that is part of the meaning of understanding. Any of us that has attempted to learn a different language also knows that the task is endless. it is instructive to compare this circularity of understanding with the circularity of scientific observation in physics.

Let us examine not how observation, facts and data are built up into general systems of physical explanation, but how these systems are built into our observations, and our appreciation of facts.

Another way to conceive understanding of the natural sciences is connected with the idea of representation. The meaning of something is a representation of that something. The term "representation" is here used in two different but closely interrelated meanings. Re-presentation means that in representing something we make that something present again. It may be present as mental content (e.g. image, concept, etc.) or it may be re-presented in the sense of "displayed in front of us." The second meaning is close to the sense of representation in a work of art (e.g. a painting or a play).

None of these meanings implies here the sense of an iconic copy. Neither our mental representations nor the "displays" of the works of art are copies of independently existing originals. Both ways of using the term "representation" refer to the constructive processes by which we try to penetrate, appropriate and display the meaning of the represented item. (von (Glasersfeld 1983, 1986). This meaning is not a disembodied quality but always a meaning to us. A copy may be an altogether bad representation making opaque the sense of the represented thing. If Picasso had "copied faithfully" (assuming that would be possible) the massacre of Guernica he would certainly not have achieved the force and depth of meaning represented in his "Guernica."

We understand something in so far as we are able to produce or interpret an adequate representation of it. Once we have discarded the notion of representations as "iconic pictures" of something external both producing and interpreting are constructive processes of the thinking subject. (von Glasersfeld 1983, 1986).

Another characteristic of this notion of understanding is that the idea of a completely right or completely wrong representation ceases to make sense. No representation is ever totally adequate because it has always limitations. On the other hand any representation has always something to tell us about the represented thing. In the limits of any representation we confront once again the impossibility of as complete grasp of a form of life. Whenever we are representing something we are also concealing some parts or aspects of that something.

The limitations and the adequacies of any representation are never known in advance, only when the representation is used (e.g. to communicate). In constructing and using representations we come to understand and as we come to understand we construct more meaningful representations. Meaningfulness is here conceived referred to the contexts and purposes of construction and use of the representation. As soon as it is used in other contexts and for other purposes anything can happen, namely problem.

The problems we encounter with our representations are not to be avoided or repressed, they should be used as the occasions to look critically at the representation. These problems may point to weak points of an otherwise useful and elegant representation. Rutherford's model of the atom was a quite elegant way of subsuming a whole array of data from physics and chemistry. It could not justify both why atoms were stable and why their spectra were discontinuous. Bohr's model did away with the first difficulty by erecting it into a postulate and explained the second for hydrogen not only with elegance but also quantitative exactness. It too failed when trying to explain more complex atoms. Problems with a representation may also arise from difficulties inherent to the complexity or elusiveness of the represented item. The representations of human cognition may be a good example. Another source of problems may come from ideas implicitly embedded in the representation but not explicitly dealt with. The representation of the cell functions with "factory models" may conceal the fairly complex interrelations and mutual influences of each organelle on all the others because it privileges hierarchical relations.

Finally, since no representation is totally adequate in principle, understanding is also connected with multiplicity of representations. To understand ideas, concept or practices of the natural sciences in a rich way we must deal with multiple representations of them. The represent understanding of the natural sciences only by knowledge of ideas, concepts, etc. is an altogether inadequate representation because it privileges products and forgets the processes of production not to mention that both products and processes are carried in specific social networks.

Natural sciences are full of representations. As a matter of fact, the natural sciences work almost exclusively with models and models of models. Some models, like the model of the atom are mechanical models of mathematical models or mathematical models built from mechanical models that subsume a great deal of empirical facts. There are models in the natural sciences that represent the not only scientific content but social and political ideas current at the time of their origin. One has only to think about the model of the cell where ideas about division of labor and management are embedded. The idea of competition as a way to success and social progress current in England through the Industrial Revolution is embodied in the concepts of natural selection and the whole framework of the theory of evolution. (Bernal 1953/1970). Interestingly enough the project of building a theory of evolution based on the concept of cooperation attempted by Kropotkine (1925) never called much attention.

Understanding scientific ideas is being able to produce different representations of them, interpret various forms of their representation and also point the limitations of each. Understanding these ideas is also knowing and analyzing the representation that have been used for them and the contexts of practice and discourse where they arose.

We can also conceive understanding as application. This conception comes from the hermeneutic tradition. Hans-Georg Gadamer, one of the foremost contemporary scholars in hermeneutic philosophy, in his major work, *Truth and Method* (1975), explicitly states that:

> "understanding always involves something like the application of the text to be understood to the present situation of the interpreter.

Understanding the natural sciences is applying them in some way to our present situation.

The idea of application we are tying to explicate here is fundamentally different from "application" in the sense commonly used in science education. The common usage originates in technological conceptions of science use and was given the status of a pedagogical instrument in Bloom's Taxonomy (Bloom 1956). Application was conceived there as the use of a general law or statement to explain or solve a concrete case. This notion was elevated to a philosophical rule of method in the deductive—nomological models of scientific explanation usually associated with logical empiricism. (Hemper 1965).

Once again we do not understand something in a general way and then apply it to something particular. We understand both the general and the particular in the very process of applying them to our present situation. Gadamer (1975) is very clear about this when he says:

> The interpreter dealing with a traditional text seeks to apply it to himself. But this does not mean that the text is given for him as something universal, that he understands it as such and only afterwards uses it for particular applications. Rather, the interpreter seeks no more than to understand this universal thing, the text; i.e. to understand what this piece of tradition says, what constitutes the meaning and importance of the text. In order to understand that, he must not seek to disregard himself and his particular hermeneutical situation. He must relate the text to this situation, if he wants to understand at all.

In the act of understanding both what we want to understand and what we apply it to, change their meaning. Application is conceived not as a deductive process (as Bloom conceives it) but as a dialogue mediated through the interpreter (i.e. the person who wants to understand).

Understanding a scientific idea, concept, formula, problem, etc. is then applying it to the relevant situation. Finding (or making) the relevant situation is already part of the application because the situations where something applies or does not are part of its meaning.

Laboratory work can be thought of as providing many occasions where application in the sense above may happen. We must remind ourselves that, conceived in this way, laboratory is not just illustration or demonstration of a concept, but rather an occasion to refine our understanding of the concept and reconceiving the practical problem at hand. Moreover, most scientific concepts have laboratory operations as part of their meaning. On the other hand the laboratory itself, the instruments contained therein, and the practices scientist engage in there are "materialized theories" to borrow an apt metaphor of Bachelar (1934/1949). The theoretical ladenness of the laboratory is vividly portrayed by Pierre Duhem when he writes :

> Enter a laboratory; approach the table crowded with an assortment of apparatus, an electric cell, silk-covered copper wire, small cups of mercury, spools, a mirror mounted on an iron bar; the experimenter is inserting into small openings the metal ends of ebony-headed pins; the iron oscillates, and the mirror attached to it throws a luminous band upon a celluloid scale; the forward-backward motion of this spot enables the physicist to observe the minute oscillations of the iron bar. Bust ask him what he is doing. Will he answer: 'I am studying the oscillations of an iron bar which carries a mirror'? No, he will say that he is measuring the electric resistance of the spools. If you are astonished, if you ask him what his words mean, what relation they have with the phenomena he has been observing and which you have noted at the same time as he, he will answer that your question requires a long explanation and that you should take a course in electricity.

Summarizing we can say that understanding what something means is a never ending process of using that something in discourse, constructing representations of it and making it relevant to our present situation. In this process, the thing to be understood, the situation in which the understanding is taking place, and the interpreter change. Another characteristic of understanding is that it happens in a social historical matrix. We understand with the tools of our culture (e.g. language.), with our previous experience (mainly our prejudices) and within the interpretive norms of specific communities.

> For a scientific mind, all knowing is an answer to a question. If there was no question, there cannot be scientific knowledge. Nothing is self-evident. Nothing is given. Everything is constructed.

Conceiving understanding of the natural sciences as the use of specific modes discourse, the production and interpretation of representations, and application in the hermeneutic sense raises two sets of questions. The first has to do with completeness. Are these aspects all there is to understand about understanding? Certainly not, understanding is too rich to be reduced to three aspects. We only touched these because they seemed important and worth exploring. The second set has to do with the practices and processes by which we may come to understand some domain of experience, namely the natural sciences.

Exploring the process of understanding we can say that it starts with "a question". We understand something in so far as we know the question that something is an answer to.

> We can say, with Collingwood (1939/1982) , that we understand only when we understand the question to which something is an answer, and it is true that what is understood in this way does not remain detached in its meaning from our own meaning. Rather, the reconstruction of the question, from which the meaning of a text is to be understood as an answer, passes into our own questioning. For the text must be understood as an answer to a real question.

Understanding starts with a question, not any question but a real question. A question that because it is real does not remain detached from us. A real question supposes that a real person (i.e. a questioner) is asking about some domain of experience (i.e. an object). Said in another way areal question expresses a desire to know. This desire is what moves the questioner to pursue the question until and adequate answer has been found (i.e. made). Desiring to know opens ourselves to experiencing what is new as new and the already known as renewed under different aspects.

A real question seems to exclude immediately both the rhetorical and the pedagogical question. (Gadamer 1975). They do not express a genuine desire to know. There is an inherent paradox in this exclusion. Rhetorical and pedagogical questions comprise most of the questions asked in school situations. The implication seems to be that genuine understanding is excluded from schools and classrooms..... unless we try to remake our ways of questioning, thus reopening the possibility of understanding in those contexts. This is not easy task, and surely it is a dangerous one.

Wherefrom do these genuine questions spring? The answer that hermeneutics gives has the sound of a provocation. They spring from our prejudices. This is surely an answer to provoke thought. Prejudices, in the original sense of pre-judgments (i.e. judgments made before all the evidence is available) are the conditions of our understanding of the world. In trying to understand science we bring to it the prejudices handed down to us by our personal history, the tradition of our communities, and history of science itself. Prejudices, in this sense, are not impediments. They are the only points from where to start our questioning. (Gadamer 1975).

Student prejudices in the form of cultural or individual conceptions are the very condition of their understanding. The students' knowledge of their world claims a wisdom and a rationality that our reverence for science has difficulty in accepting. Instead of engaging with students in the questioning of our prejudices, and the prejudices of science we try to erase the students knowledge. With the best of intenti ns we strip ourselves from the possibility of understanding science and in the process transform it into a sort of alien dogma.

Questions, if they are genuine cannot be asked from a detached stance. The disembodied observer that asks the questions of science is a fantasy of the worst kind because it obscures the human side of science. Scientists, like everyone else, ask their questions in the context of their research traditions and within communities of practice and discourse. Even revolutions in science exhibit many continuities with their ancestors. Our questions if they are going to be ways of understanding have to be asked from the hic et nunc of our interpretive situation.

Questions and prejudices help us see understanding as an inherently historical process. We can understand the natural sciences in so far as we are part of the same historical continuity. Our own culture and our own personal history are in some ways continuous with these sciences. Understanding the natural sciences is not only an attempt at understanding a domain of experience but also an attempt at understanding ourselves (both at personal and cultural levels). (Gadamer 1975).

Inherent continuities must not make us forget the inherent discontinuities. The otherness that asserts itself in the natural sciences is a constant invitation to our efforts of understanding and a constant warning against hasty interpretation. We understand the

natural sciences in so far as, from our prejudices, our history, our culture, we relentlessly pursue their subject matter, what they are about. The subject matter is understandable only because we question these forms of life. At the same time the meaning that our understanding achieves, emerges because we question the natural sciences with our prejudices (i.e. expectations that some meaning will emerge). Understanding the natural sciences is a constant movement between what we expect and what emerges from our questioning (Gadamer 1975).

We all know the history of Penelope, wife of Ulysses, who in order to delay her answer to marriage proposals wove a cloth during the day and unwove it during the night. Understanding the natural sciences can be conceived in these terms.

Questioning the natural sciences makes us unweave their fabric, understand not only the superficial pattern (i.e. the finished knowledge) but also the underlying frame of threads (i.e. interconnections between the ideas) and the ways in which these were woven in the first place (i.e. history and sociology of science).

The unweaving makes us also become aware of our own frames of questioning (i.e. our prejudices) and also question them from the point of view of science.

Hopefully we will achieve a new tapestry that will integrate our own views with those of the sciences without subordination but in the eye-to-eye of genuine dialogue.

The Research Problem

"Achievement in Science at +2 level"

Why this Study?

Science has occupied almost all spheres of human life an living. We are living in a society which is completely drawn into the scientific environment. Now, we can not think of a world without science. The wonderful achievements of science has glorified the modern world and transformed the modern civilization into a scientific civilization.

Science is no longer confined to a few seriously devoted persons. Since life in the present world invariably warrants, to variable degrees, knowledge of scientific facts and laws, science has now become everyday science for everybody. Teaching of everyday

science for everybody has become an unavoidable part of general education. Nobody questions its inclusion as a subject in the school curriculum. It is included in a school's curriculum for the same reasons as any other subject, but in addition science inculcates certain special values peculiar to it and which no other subject can provide. But besides satisfying the usual needs for its inclusion as a subject in the curriculum such as intellectual, cultural, moral, aesthetic, utilitarian and vocational values—science learning provides training in scientific method and also helps to develop a scientific attitude of mind in the learner. The qualities imbibed by the learner through learning science are of great value to a citizen living in the society. Hence, science is now made a compulsory subject in every system of school education right from the elementary stage.

Science teaching in schools, can and should make a difference in the lives of children and the difference should be on the positive side of the educational ladder. Much has been said about the importance of children's understanding the nature of the scientific enterprise. In a free society, scientific advancement is dependent upon the will of the people, their will as decision-making citizens to support it and their will as individuals to become scientists. Therefore, liberally educated people in a free society should understand the nature of the scientific enterprise, the social, economic, and political factors that effect its development and the personal satisfactions that come to one who pursues a career in it.

Science has been referred to as a self-corrective process of finding out. Or as Niels Bohr expressed it, 'science includes the methods by which man puts limiting values on his preconceptions'. Or as Percy bridgeman opined it, the methods of science consist of doing your demands to get the answer with no holds barred. Regardless of whether we refer to them as the methods of science, as problem solving, as inquiry or as discovery, there are processes of investigation in science that have been found to be effective in advancing our understanding of natural phenomena. Elements of the process have been defined in various ways and research has clearly indicated that pupils can be taught how to perform them in conducting their own investigations. Furthermore, as they learn to perform the process, they become more independent or self directive in their learning. To become independent in these ways

meets a basic need of all children and thus represents a kind of satisfaction that can be achieved in no other way. If properly taught, science can help all children learn how to learn.

In questions of science Galileo Galilei once said 'the authority of a thousand is not worth the humble reasoning of a single individual.' While learning science, the learner develops certain faculties through reasoning and experimentation which no other subject can provide.

Considering science from the intellectual point of view, it is the most inexhaustible storehouse of knowledge. Since Nature is an inexhaustible source of knowledge, science as a subject, offers the widest range of knowledge to the learners. It has exposed the mankind to infinite avenues of knowledge in nature, living and non-living, the world we perceive and also the world beyond human perception thereby makes us conscious of the unknown to be explored.

Science, besides satisfying the intellectual curiosity of man and providing materials and media for intellectual exercise, has disciplinary effect on the minds of individuals. Since science covers the widest range of knowledge, the learner wonders at the intricacies and mysteries of the Universe, the known and the unknown. These tend to create a broader outlook in the life of the learner.

Science is universal in character and it has no barrier of any kind. The scientific revolution began in Western Europe where modern science was born but its home is now the whole world. The fruits of scientific discoveries in one country are enjoyed by the people all over the world. Science is not concerned with caste, creed or colour nor recognizes territorial barriers. Such a pattern inherent in science will definitely have an impact on the minds of the learners and is expected to help to develop broad-mindedness in them.

The study of science has several other disciplinary values. For instance, science is an interest-awakening subject and its pursuit demands persistent efforts, diligence and patience. Any experimentation in science requires keen observation, concentration of mind as well as accurate representation of facts. There is no place for prejudice or bias in science. Scientific pursuits warrant objective observation and impartial judgement. Engagement in any scientific activity, be it theoretical or experimental, therefore, pre-supposed intellectual honesty, preserverance, concentration of mind and broad-mindedness. In science we do not conclude or predict any thing on the basis of superstition, traditional belief or hear-say, unless the facts are based on proof. In science there is no place for sentiment or emotion except rationality. A scientific result to be acceptable must be valid for all cases

In pursuing a scientific problem, one has to define the problem, plan the process, collect relevant data, formulate necessary hypotheses, repeat the processes if necessary, apply to specific cases before generalizing. During the process, one has to be logical and objective at every step. Thus, scientific pursuits demand such qualities as minute observation, scientific attitude of mind, persistence, preserverance, concentration of mind, accuracy of measurement, patience; logical, objective and unprejudiced judgement; respect for other's opinions, respect for truth, etc. These disciplinary qualities of mind, if cultivated through the teaching of science, may be carried over to manifest in the general behaviour of the learner. This will prove useful for living as an efficient social individual in the society. No other subject provides opportunities for inculcation of so many disciplinary qualities of the mind of the learners.

It is hardly necessary to elaborate the utilitarian or practical values of science. The present world is a world of science and technology. Every thing or every event happening around us demands some knowledge of simple scientific facts or principles. Without the elementary knowledge and information of science, we will be at a loss. Science is now everyday science for everybody.

The achievements and the benefits of science touch all sectors and all levels of the modern society. The modern man has applied science and technology for the well-being of mankind by inventing machines and by harnessing the resources of nature. The gifts of science have been profitably used for making life comfortable and raising the standard of living. But the use or abuse of the wonderful gifts of science depends on man and his mind. The recent advances in the field of science and technology and the wide application of the achievements of science in industry, agriculture, medicine, transport and communication as well as their uses in domestic life justify, more than ever, the utilitarian values of science.

Science has opened innumerable avenues for pursuing different vocations. A student of science can study engineering and technology, medicine, agriculture or any similar subject and make his career in that profession. In addition, scientific activities have given rise to many varieties of crafts and allied services. Science, therefore, gives opportunities for career-making and pursuing professions and vocations. In fact, if we refer to preparation of the individual for the future as one of the aims of education, then science, as a subject, is rightly serving this purpose. In this age of science and technology there is a demand for technical personnel. The maintenance and creation of new departments, new establishments need the services of engineers, scientists and technicians and there will always be need for research workers in new fields of science. Educationist Paul Fredman once said, science is no longer the preserve of a few completely—perhaps abnormally devoted men; it is becoming and increasingly will become, one of the major professions open to any young man of ability, demanding no more in the way of special bent or devotion than medicine or law. But like those other professions, it too will continue to offer a life with characteristic flavor; it will have its own professional standards and its own typical type of thinking and will call forth its practitioners its own loyalties.

Science has made a tremendous impact on the cultural life of the present day society which is a product of science. The thinking, feeling and actions of a modern man are practically guided by the effects of science. There is an involvement of science, direct or indirect, in all works as well as leisure of a modern man. Our habits and attitudes have also been affected by science.

The study of science brings behavioural change in the learner and enriches his character and personality. Science gives opportunity for creative thinking and constructive imagination. Further, science is a subject where ideas can be experimented upon and verified. The learner develops the habits of searching for the truth. These qualities affect the pattern of behaviour of the learner. The significant aspect of science is that whatever the student learns has immediate application in the world around him. This is educationally very sound.

In society, there will always be problems to be solved. One of the very useful outcomes of learning science is the development of problem solving skill. If properly cultivated through the teaching of science, the student can apply this skill to solve problems in his personal or social life.

One of the aims of modern education is to provide means for utilization of leisure especially in the industrialized societies. There is no end to interesting pursuits in science, intellectual or otherwise. Scientific activities provide the best hobbies and pass times for proper utilization or leisure.

At higher levels, arts and science are no way different. There can be no good piece of art without application of science, and on the other hand there is artistic or aesthetic element in all scientific activities. The great thinkers have always been stressing the need for the unity of science and arts, for they originate from the same root. In the modern civilization, scientific creations glorify arts and aesthetics and science may be said to be the modern substitute for arts in the sense that it is the result of the same kind of creative thought and action which have generated arts.

Arts and aesthetics are components of culture and civilization. The creation of the universe is a great piece of art. There is aesthetics in the mysteries and harmonies of nature. Saunders felt that 'there is an aesthetic side to the scientist's activities and to his contribution to human culture. On the lowest level he has the satisfaction of adding to the sum of human knowledge; on a higher level he enjoys the subtle pleasure of devising some hypothesis which fits a diversity of facts opening up new areas of knowledge. Appreciation of 'fitness of purpose', the suitability of an apparatus for the job for which it was designed, can give great inward satisfaction. There is a pleasing skill in avoiding or eliminating sources of errors and in particular the errors of human observation. Wonder is aroused by neatness with which some material quality or some living activity, can be sorted out from other qualities or activities for examination and demonstration. There is an elegance that runs through the logic and handiwork of the scientists. It is seen in the formulae of mathematicians, it is equally seen in the experiments and observations of great naturalists. The very simplicity of great generalizations of science stirs the imagination. With microscope and telescope the scientist opens up new worlds of wonder and beauty. A speck of living matter becomes a creature of incredible beauty, a snow flake more lovely than diamonds and a distant star becomes a universe. It is at this level that science shares equally with the arts; the privilege of contributing to the aesthetic development of the human race.

Culture in addition to knowledge, includes all activities, thoughts, feelings, attitudes, patterns of individual or social life of men. The study of science gives opportunity for the development of favourable traits of human character which become a positive contribution to the cultural life of the society. For instance, with science gaining ground and spreading its influence in the life of man, there has been a profusion of literature based in science. Scientific fiction, being interesting, adds to the cultural heritage of man. Similarly, the literature on history and development of science is no less interesting. It is the study of the origin and development of civilization itself and has developed into a separate branch of study which contributes to the cultural heritage.

The biographies of scientists incorporated in the science course develop a scientific attitude among the learners. The description of the pursuits of scientists, their tenacity and preserverance, etc., are worth reading. Such a study brings out the scientists' attitude towards science and their hopes and frustrations on their way to discovery. Sometimes, even after their invention or discovery, it takes a long time for social acceptance. The facts about the sacrifices of the scientists for the benefit of mankind stir one's imagination. The lives of Galileo, Watt, Curies and others show how the scientist has to suffer to make an original discovery. The lives of the scientists can inspire the minds of the young learners. It is believed that the study of science and the life of the scientists engenders praise worthy humility.

The study of the scientist's way of discovery is more interesting. It gives the learners an opportunity to grasp the essential steps of scientific method or procedure. For example, the story of the discovery of the Laws of Gravity by Sir Isaac Newton or the story of the discovery of the cause of malaria by Sir Ronald Ross, wili help to make the meaning of science clear. It is useful to give the pupils, the idea how scientists sacrifice their personal comfort for the good of society. Broad-mindedness and selfless service to mankind are characteristics of their lives.

A scientist is a seeker of truth and scientific facts give a true picture of nature. In a scientific pursuit, it requires intellectual honesty at each step. In an experiment, one has to record correct data, collect authentic information and make objective interpretation of observations. Any thing other than truth will lead to wrong results. For exploration of the unknown, scientists have to proceed carefully on the basis of the true picture at each stage of the process. Intellectual honesty and love for truth coupled with sincerity of purpose and virtues are prerequisites in any scientific pursuit. In science ultimately truth prevails, because science is nothing, but truth. There can be no better moral value of a subject than this virtue.

Considering the importance, as explained, the achievement in science was taken into consideration for a detailed study. The results of this present study will help in bringing out the remedial measures for the failures every year in the Intermediate Public Examinations.

Objectives

The following objectives were framed for the present research study.

1. To find out the level of achievement in science at +2 level.
2. To compare the achievement in science of Intermediate students studying in residential and non-residential colleges.
3. To compare the achievement in science of Intermediate students studying in private and government colleges.
4. To compare the achievement in science of Intermediate boys and girls.

Scope and Limitations

In the present study, the science is confined to physics and chemistry for the purpose of collection of marks to measure the achievement of Intermediate students. Residential and non-residential colleges, private and government colleges, and boys and girls are the variables of the study. This study covers some colleges throughout the state, Andhra Pradesh. There are neither controlled groups nor experimental groups. Intervening variables are not taken into consideration.

Related Literature

Any worthwhile research study in any field of knowledge requires an adequate familiarity with the work which has already been done in the same area. A summary of the writings of recognized authorities and of previous research provides evidence that the research is familiar with what is already known and what is still unknown and untested. Since effective research is based upon past knowledge, this step helps to eliminate the duplication of what has been done, and provides useful hypotheses and helpful suggestions for significant investigation (Best, 1982).

Citing studies that show substantial agreement and those that seem to present conflicting conclusions help to sharpen and define understanding of existing knowledge in the problem area, provides a background for the research project, and makes the investigator aware of the status of the issue. Parading a long list of annotated studies relating to the problem is ineffective and inappropriate. Only those studies that are plainly relevant, competently executed, and clearly reported should be included.

In searching related literature, the researcher should note certain important elements. They include—

1. Reports of closely related studies that have been investigated.
2. Design of the study, including procedures employed, and data-gathering instruments used,

3. Populations that were sampled and sampling methods employed,
4. Variables that were defined,
5. Extraneous variables that could have affected the findings,
6. Faults that could have been avoided, and
7. Recommendations for further research.

Capitalizing on the reviews of expert researchers can be fruitful in providing helpful ideas and suggestions. While review articles that summarize related studies are useful. They do not provide a satisfactory substitute for an independent work, it is one of the first steps in the research process. Hence this collection of literature about the importance and objectives of science/biology teaching and about the related research studies.

Education Commission (1964-66) stated that Science education must become an integral part of school education; and ultimately some study of science should become a part of all courses in the humanities and social sciences. The quality of science teaching is to be developed considerably so as to achieve its proper objectives and purposes. *viz.*, to understand basic principles; to develop problem-solving. Analytical skills and ability; to apply them to the problems of material environments and social living besides promoting the spirit of enquiry and experimentation. Science strengthens commitments of man to free enquiry and search for truth as its highest duty and obligation. By its emphasis on reason and free enquiry, it even helps to lesson ideological tensions.

Although science is largely occupied with the understanding of Nature of present, its development is tending more and more to help man to understand himself and his place in the world in such developments. The commission observes that the pursuit of mere material affluence and power would be subordinated to that of higher values and the fulfillment of the needs of individual. This concept of mingling of science and spirituality is of special significance of Indian Education.

It is commonly felt that a child's education cannot be complete unless he has some knowledge of science irrespective of the field of study he wishes to pursue in latter life. Today the great advances in science rendered it absolutely necessary that a fundamental knowledge of science should be the 'sine qua non' of any person who was educated and who wished to lead a life which combined in itself something of scientific aspects of existence.

Objectives in any areas of curriculum should be regarded as the directions of growth and not as the ultimate ends to be completely reached. In this respect, science is not different from other branches. It is important that objectives should be selected towards which the growth and development of the individual may be directed from a very practical point of view. Objectives need to be selected and stated in such a way that progress towards their attainment may be appraised (Heiss, Oboum and Hoffman, 1950).

A judicious formulation and selection of worthwhile objectives for any school subject goes a long way in enriching and shaping both the teaching and testing in that subject and such objectives should be evolved in relation to the needs of the individual in his society. The three main sources for the formulation of the objectives are—

(1) the needs and capabilities of the pupil,

(2) the specific demands of his social environment, and

(3) the nature of the subject matter.

Science teachers have long recognized the need for sound objectives in curriculum planning. In an examination of over 3,000 statements written from 1901 to 1950 by secondary school teachers, Paul Hurd (1954) noted that the objectives of science teaching were the teacher's first consideration in planning curriculum. Objective strongly influence the organization of the curriculum and at the same time they provide the guidelines on the selection of teaching techniques.

National society for the study of Education in its Yearbook (1947) published the objectives under these categories, *viz.*

(1) functional information of habits.

(2) functional concepts.

(3) functional understanding of principles.

(4) instrumental skills,

(5) problem solving skills,

(6) attitudes,

(7) appreciations, and

(8) interests.

Bloom. *et al.* (1959) classified the educational objectives under three domains, *viz.*, the cognitive, the effective, and the psychomotor. The cognitive domain includes those objectives which deal with the recall or recognition of knowledge and the development of intellectual abilities and skills. The affective domain includes objectives which describe changes in interests, attitudes, values, and the development of appreciations and adequate adjustment. The work done in that period on manipulative or motor-skill was very less which includes motor activities.

Rai (1975) in his report on school Science Teaching stated that the main objectives for teaching of science should be—

1. To arouse the curiosity of the student about the world we live in and to encourage him to understand the various natural phenomena.
2. To train to acquire that habit of making observation in a planned way.
3. To develop in him science attitude.
4. To give him an idea how a scientist works.

The aims and objectives of teaching general science according to All India Seminar on Teaching of Science (1963) should be—

1. To familiarize the pupil with the world in which he lives and make him understand the impact of science on society so as to enable him to adjust himself to his environment.
2. To acquaint him with the scientific method and enable him to develop scientific attitude.
3. To give the pupil a historical perspective, so that he may understand the evolution of scientific development.

The Directorate of Extension programmes for Secondary education, Government of India, in its brochure on 'Evaluation in General Science' sets some of the objectives of teaching general science in secondary schools as—

1. The pupils studying general science should acquire knowledge of the fundamentals of science useful to all in everyday life.
2. They should develop the ability to apply the knowledge in everyday life.
3. They should acquire experimental skills such as :
   (*a*) handing apparatus and instruments;
   (*b*) arranging apparatus for an experiment; and

(*c*) preserving apparatus, chemicals, specimens, models, etc.

4. They should acquire constructional skills such as ;
   (*a*) improvising simple instruments and appliances, and
   (*b*) repairing certain instruments and appliances of every-day life.
5. They should develop drawing skills such as:
   (*a*) drawing and sketching certain objects, instrument sand arrangements; and
   (*b*) photography in certain objects and specimens.
6. They should be able to locate reliable and recent information from appropriate sources.
7. They should be able to interpret scientific data given in various forms such as tabular, graphical, scientific, etc.
8. They should develop the power of minute observation of their surroundings.
9. They should develop the power of oral expression in science to discuss, argue, describe and raise questions using scientific terminology.
10. They should develop the scientific method in thinking and action.
11. They should adopt the scientific attitude in making statements, accepting information and forming beliefs.
12. They should develop interest in scientific reading and hobbies.
13. They should be able to appreciate the impact of science on life, bath personal and social, the struggle through which science has advanced, and the inspiring works of the scientists.

The following similar set of objectives was formulated by the principals of Delhi Higher Secondary Schools in the third summer camp organized by the extension department of the Central Institute of Education, Delhi.

1. To develop in the student a scientific attitude.
2. To develop in the student critical thinking.
3. To enable the student to acquire the fundamentals of scientific method.

4. To develop in the student skill in laboratory techniques.
5. To enable the student to be creative.
6. To develop in the student the ability to apply scientific knowledge and principles to problems of everyday life and new situations.
7. To enable the student to comprehend scientific terms, concepts, symbols, various tables and their uses.
8. To enable the student to construct and interpret graphs, diagrams and models.
9. To enable the student to collect and interpret data for the solution of problems.
10. To enable the student to be familiar with the natural resources of his environment and their uses.
11. To enable the student to be familiar with the trends in modern science.
12. To enable the student to appreciate the beauty and order in nature.

Approach paper on science and mathematics in General Education (1985) developed by NCERT thought of the possibility of fulfilling the following objectives for secondary level for enabling the students—

1. To study a few aspects of physical and life sciences in detail with a special emphasis on those areas of concern like food, shelter, health, energy, nutrition, and major components of environment;
2. To appreciate the need of quantification in the scientific students;
3. To develop in science and ability to put the interest into action;
4. To manipulate tools, equipment in a proper manner;
5. To identify the factors operating in the environment; and
6. To collect data, classify and draw reasonable inferences.

These objectives of secondary stage are to be fulfilled along with the objectives of primary and middle stages which include - collection of information; classification of objects, events, etc.; identification of cause and effect relationship; development of scientific attitudes; acquainting with natural phenomena; giving emphasis to the relevance of science to daily life, etc.

Bhaskara Rao (1989) stated that a teacher must formulate some definite objectives and specifications. . . . in order to achieve desirable behavioural changes among pupils. He emphasized on objectives such as knowledge, understanding, application, skill, interest, scientific attitudes, and appreciation.

The objectives of science explained by various individuals, commissions and conferences are concerned to biology also. Certain specific objectives are also developed only for biology. Let us observe then now.

First Asian Regional conference on school Biology (1966) held at Manila recommended the following aims and objectives of school biology teaching in Asia.

1. To develop and instil in student the scientific attitude of inquiry and experimentation.
2. To provide sufficient understanding of the concepts of biology to enable students to become worthy citizens of the world.
3. To provide the opportunities for a practical understanding of the method of biologists which give them confidence to attempt the solution of problems which they have to face in their individual and social lives.
4. To give the student the incentive to pursue the study at higher levels of biology and related fields.
5. To encourage respect and feeling for living things.

And the latest national Policy on education—1986 states that 'Science Education will be strengthened so as to develop in the child well defined abilities and values such as the spirit of inquiry, creativity, objectivity, the courage to question, and on aesthetic sensibility.

All the above aims and objectives of science stress, directly or indirectly, the importance of scientific attitude, scientific aptitude, skills, abilities and interests. And also we can sense that a pupil of biology should be in a position to utilize his classroom learning in daily life through proper achievement and application.

Academic achievement is of paramount importance, particularly in the present socio-economic and cultural contexts. Obviously, in the school, great emphasis is placed on achievement right from the beginning of the formal education. The school has its own systematic hierarchy which is largely based on achievement and performance rather than aspiration or quality. Thus, the school tends to emphasize achievement which facilitates, among other things, the process of role allocation for the social system. The school performs the function of selection and differentiation among students on the basis of their scholastic and other attainments and opens out avenues for advancement, again, primarily in terms of achievement.

A considerable number of students from school go to colleges and institutions of higher learning. It is very important to ensure that such students acquire the requisite competence so as to benefit most out of higher education. Setting the stage for the achievement of the youth is thus a fundamental obligation of the educational system of the school stage.

Science is one of the compulsory subjects in the school curriculum in Andhra Pradesh. It paves way to the career deciding courses at +2, stage. The acquisition of the knowledge of science terms, principles and concepts, a clear understanding of them, the ability to use such knowledge in different situations in life and in the development of skills should be the outcomes of teaching and learning of science. Moreover, the students should develop a proper attitude towards the study of science and an active interest in the subject, besides appreciating the importance of science in human life and civilization. All these should be assessed by terminal examinations conducted of the end of each class.

The results of class X in Andhra Pradesh have not been crossing 40-45 per cent for many years. Statistics show that many a pupil fall in science which includes biology as one of its constituents along with physics and chemistry. Let us see the other research results in the field of achievement in science.

Second International Science Study (1988) in its study concluded that the science achievement scores of fifth grade in sixteen participating countries (viz. Australia, Canada, England, Finland, Hong Kong, Hungary, Italy, Japan, Korea, Netherlands, Norway, Philippines, Poland, Singapore, Sweden, Thailand, and United States of America) were about the same in 1986 as in 1970. There was a drop in achievement from 1970 to 1986 in the ninth grade.

The growth in science achievement from grade five to grade nine was less in 1986 than in 1970.

Science achievement in the ninth grade for sixteen countries, according to the second International science Study. Hungary had the highest mean science achievement score in grade nine. The ninth grade students had difficulty with items that required such higher order logical skills as analysis, application, and mental model building. Contrary to this, Williams (1987) found that the pupils achievement was poor in respect of the understanding and knowledge objectives compared to that in respect of the skill and application objectives of teaching general science in high schools.

According to the same Second International science Study. When ranked with 15 participating countries it was found that Japan, Korea, and Finland had the highest science achievement scores in grade five. The U.S. students had difficulty in reading a table and identifying a change over time. There was small gain from 1970 on items that were classified as 'process' items and a small decline on 'non-process' items.

Patnaik (1986) tried to measure the achievement in general science of Class V pupils. She found that the pupils of U.P. schools were much superior to those of M.E. schools. And at the same time she also found that the pupils of municipality schools were superior to those in the schools under D.I. of schools at 95 per cent confidence level.

Second International Science Study had a significant comparative study about biology achievement in thirteen countries. The First Year Biology Test with 30 items was administered to 2,582 students in 118 schools of 13 countries. The Advanced Science Biology Test was given to 674 second year biology students in 43 secondary schools. This reflected a response rate of over 80 per cent of the schools contacted. The 'mean per cent correct' of biology students who had two or more years of biology education are compared with the scores of students of 13 other countries along with the U.S. The results of this study were : Students in the U.S. who had studied biology for two years ranked 13th among 13 countries in achievement in biology. singapore had the highest mean achievement score in biology. Students of the U.S. with 2 years of biology scored about 10 per cent higher than students who had one year of biology.

Sundararajan (1989) found that the higher secondary boys studying in urban schools did not show greater achievement in biology than the boys studying in rural schools.

The higher secondary school girls studying in urban schools showed greater achievement in biology than the girls studying in rural schools (Sundararajan, 1989). This was in agreement with the findings of Das (1985), and there were significant differences in respect of understanding and application of objectives of science (Williams, 1987).

The boys studying in urban schools did not show greater achievement in biology than girls studying in the urban schools (Sundararajan, 1989) But Saxena (1963) found contrary in his study.

The higher secondary school boys studying in rural schools showed greater achievement in biology than the girls studying in rural schools (Sundararajan). This is in agreement with the finding of Williams (1979).

The group performance of boys was superior to that of the girls in all branches (Thakur, 1972). This was in agreement with the result in the U. S. where at all grade levels and in all science subjects, boys had higher science achievement than girls.

Contrary to the findings, in grade five, the Philippines had the smallest male-female difference in mean achievement in science (Jacobson and Doran, 1988). In grade nine, Hungary and the Philippines had the smallest male-female difference in science achievement (Jacobson and Doran). And it was also observed that the mean scores of boys and girls differ significantly only for subjects with unfavourable attitude (Sumangala, 1986).

Biology was the only subject, in some countries, in which girls scored higher than boys. in chemistry, Sweden had the smallest male-female difference in achievement. In physics, England had the smallest difference between male and female scores. This study concluded that the difference between boys and girls in science achievement was greater in the physical sciences than in the life sciences (Jacobson and Doran).

In the U. S., there were greater differences between schools in biology achievement than those in any other country. Apparently, in the U.S., the students chances of doing well in biology, to a large extent, were dependent upon the school he attended (Jacobson and Doran).

Swamamma (1987) observed that the achievement in biology of upper primary school pupils was not quite satisfactory' will throw light on the poor results of the secondary education.

Ebel (1938) stated that a scientific attitude is an attitude which will tend to foster scientific achievement.

Bhaskara Rao (1989) identified a high positive association between scientific attitude and biology achievement in secondary school pupils.

The association among scientific attitude, scientific aptitude and biology achievement in both boys and girls was highly significant and positive,. The association between scientific attitude and biology achievement was more and the association between scientific aptitude and biology achievement was relatively less in boys. The same trend was seen in the case of girls too (Bhaskara Rao, 1989).

The association between scientific attitude and biology achievement in the pupils studying in private and government secondary schools was highly and positively significant (Bhaskara Rao, 1989), but the association was less in private schools.

A positively significant association was observed by Bhaskara Rao (1989) between scientific attitude and achievement in biology in urban and rural secondary pupils, but it was high in urban pupils.

There was a high positive association between scientific attitude and achievement in biology in English and Telugu medium pupils (Bhaskara Rao. 1989) but it was very high in telugu medium pupils.

A significant positive association was observed between scientific attitude and achievement in biology in residential and non-residential school pupils, but it was high in residential schools (Bhaskara Rao, 1989).

To Sir Francis Galton, a scientific attitude was 'an inherent stimulus to climb the path that leads to knowledge with the strength to reach the summit—one which, if hindered and thwarted, will fret and strive until all hindrance is overcome, and it is again free to follow its labour-loving instinct (Young and Schmid, 1968).

Crawford with Stanford Scientific Aptitude Test reported a correlation of 0.3 between scores earned on this test by entering students and their first year grades or marks in science and pre-engineering courses. In support of this finding, Bennett, Seashore and Wesman (Rethinking science Education, 1960), the constructors of the differential aptitude Tests, found that the success in science shows highest correlation with verbal reasoning, numerical ability and certain aspects of language of aptitude. The Guilford-Zimmerman aptitude Survey (1950) also revealed that there was a significant relationship between science achievement and scientific aptitude.

Pillai (1986), Jose (1987), Sujatha (1987), Thampy (1984) and Nair and Joseph (1978) in their studies found that there was a significant positive influence by scientific aptitude on biology achievement.

Bhaskara Rao (1989) identified a positive association between scientific attitude and achievement in biology at secondary school level. But this association was less when compared with the association between scientific aptitude and achievement in biology.

The influence of scientific aptitude on the achievement of pupils with different levels of scientific aptitude was different, and the scientific aptitude was highly influencing the biology achievement of the pupils with average scientific aptitude (Jose. 1987).

Studies of Ganguly, *et al.* (1972). Nair and Joseph (1978) and Skaria (1984) revealed that scientific aptitude was highly associated with academic success in science achievement of girls.

A low, but positively significant, association between scientific aptitude and achievement in biology was identified in both boys and girls (Bhaskara Rao, 1989). Bhasakara Rao (1989) identified a significantly high positive association between scientific aptitude and achievement in biology in private schools.

The differences between means of the sub-urban under-achievers and over-achievers on the composite aptitude test were significant and the means were in favour of the under-achievers whereas there was no significant difference in the aptitude scores of rural and urban over—and under-achievers (Mitra, Chatterji and Mukherji, 1975).

Bhaskara Rao (1989) identified a significantly high positive association between scientific attitude in both urban and rural pupils, but it was high in urban pupils.

There was a positive association between scientific aptitude and achievement in biology in English and Telugu medium pupils, but it was high in telugu medium secondary school pupils (Bhaskara Rao, 1989).

A positively significant association was seen between scientific aptitude and achievement in biology in non-residential school pupils (Bhaskara Rao, 1989).

Pillai (1986), Thakur (1972) and Joseph (1987) found that there was a significant positive relationship between science achievement, scientific aptitude and intelligence.

Sreekumar (1972). Chatterji, et al. (1978) and Sujatha (1987) identified the positive relationship between scientific aptitude, science interest and science achievement.

General ability. scientific aptitude/reasoning, problem solving ability were significantly responsible for the learning of science (pal. 1982).

The studies of Zyve (1929), Berton and Perry (1975) on predictive value of Stanford scientific aptitude Test found that the scientific aptitude can be employed for predicting science achievement.

Science achievement has a significant role to play in predicting scientific aptitude (Gupta, 1985). For scientific aptitude, both achievement and information in the scientific fields may be prerequisites for mastery over the basic scientific skills which in turn, would lead to the unfolding of other mental abilities.

Clark (1927) found that students whose parents had college education ranked higher in scholarship. Shuttleworth (1927) reported that the low-achieving group of students had strict religious home training.

Bear (1928) found that parental occupation was related to academic success. He reported that sons of farmers and businessmen ranked low in scholarship in comparison with those of artisans, salesmen and so on.

Austin (1964) found very high relationship between the tendency to drop out of college and parents' education and father's occupation. sinha (1970), and Wig and Nagpal (1970) found that low achievers represented more in occupational category-agricultural or business.

Griffits (1926) found a close relationship between school grades and family size, children from small families were found superior in school grades.

Havighurst (1964) contrasted achievement test performance of middle- class and lower- class children in 21 Chicago school districts. He found that 6th grade students in the seven districts with the highest average socio-economic status ranged from grade level to one year above grade level in reading and mathematics tests; in the seven lowest socio-economic status districts, the scores clustered around one year below grade level.

Mishra, Das and Padhi (1960) reported a correlation of 0.59 between home environment and school achievement whereas correlation of 0.31 between intelligence test scores and school achievement.

Menon (1973) found over-achievement and under-achievement are highly influenced by socio-economic status. Anand (1973) established relationship between socio-economic status and academic achievement even when the influence of intelligence of non-verbal and verbal type was partialled out. He also found that the impact of socio-economic environment was found to influence mental abilities and academic achievement.

Abraham (1974) found achievement level in English is associated with socic-economic status and Basavayya (1974) observed that overall language achievement is influenced by the parental occupation and education.

A study on difficulties in learning English by Dewal (1974) revealed that effective teaching and learning are hampered by poor socio-economic background.

Bhaduri (1971) observed that the over-achievers showed higher scores in study habits, attitude to school, and religious-cultural background; the under-achievers on the contrary, tended to have a higher socio-economic status, a more congenial home condition and more of leisure time activities.

Lalithamma (1975) found that the achievement in mathematics was positively related to intelligence, study habits, interest in mathematics and socio-economic status. Correlation between socio-economic status and academic achievement as computed by Chandra (1975) was reported as positive and is supported by Homchandhuri (1980).

Satyanandam (1969) highlighted two sub-aspects of socio-economic status, *viz.*, educational level of parents and economic status of parents. According to him, the children of graduate parents performed far better than the children of matriculate parents.

Children of upper and lower, upper and middle economic strata only differed significantly on the variable of achievement (Anand and Padma, 1987). Chatterji, Mukherjee and Banerjee (1971) also found that parent's education level was directly related to the achievement of their children.

Khanna (1980) observed that the academic achievement of the children of educated parents, illiterate parents, and educated mothers was significantly correlated with the socio-economic status of the family. Menon (1972) also noticed that higher occupational and educational level of father, educational level of mother, family income and parental attention were related to high achievement.

Ojha (1979) concluded that higher the socio-economic status the better would be the academic achievement at high school level. Parental education, occupation, and income were also related with the educational achievement of both rural and urban boys of 9th class.

Choudhari (1975) expressed an opinion based on research that bright children normally came from families where parents having a higher level of education, were mostly engaged in professions requiring general knowledge, and had more income than the parents of dull students. In Goswami's (1978) study also the scholastic achievement correlated highly with socio-economic status.

Goswami (1982) found a significant relationship between socio-economic status and reading interests and also between reading interests and academic achievement.

Jain (1981) states that the socio-economic level of the parents had a great impact on the pupil's achievement in Gujarati language, social studies, science and mathematics. The pupils belonging to the upper socio-economic status achieved better than the pupils whose parents belonged to the middle and lower socio-economic levels, while the pupils from the middle socio-economic levels scored better than those with lower socio-economic status of the parents, in all the subjects. Academic achievement (Tripathi) had a high positive correlation with socio-economic status.

Family background factors of college students, according to Siddiqui (1979), had positive relationship with the academic achievement of the students when the intelligence factor was held constant. Somesundaram observed that the variables which discriminated between the unselected groups of normal and under-achievers were social standards, introversion and family relations.

Griffits (1926) observed that within the family the older and the younger children tended to perform about equally well scholastically. Gupta (1982) found that birth order and the father's profession influenced the reading ability (in Hindi) of children studying in classes III and IV.

Chatterji, *et. al.* (1971) concluded that the family size and the number of siblings were inversely related, especially in low intellectual level. Dave and Dave (1971) observed that the size of the family was not related to the academic achievement.

Dave and Dave (1971) noticed that a higher percentage of rank students belonged to homes having higher parental income, occupation and education, whereas a higher percentage of failed students belonged to homes having lower parental income, occupation and education.

In the study of Dhami (1974) the relationship between socio-economic status and academic achievement, though statistically significant, was not very high. Socio-economic status was moderately correlated with achievement in the study of Srivastava (1980). Sinha (1970) also observed only small differences on their parent's education and father's education. The socio-economic status of the pupils' parents was not significantly related to scholastic performance at class VIII and Class IX but at class X the pupils hailing from homes with higher socio-economic status performed better (Reddy, 1981)

Nemzek (1940) reported that education of parents and their profession have no influence over the academic success of their children. But for the high ability group, children of servicemen excelled the children of businessmen, and the trend was reversed for the average and low intellectual groups (Chatterji Mukherjee and Banerjee).

Salunke (1979) found no relationship between socio-economic status and achievement. Bhat and Indiresan (1981) failed to draw definite conclusions regarding the differential performance of students belonging to different socio-economic backgrounds as the sample consisted mainly of students belonging to the backward class and low-income group.

Chatterji, Mukherjee and Banerjee (1971) concluded that the economic conditions of the family seemed to have no effect upon the scholastic achievement in all the intellectual ability groups. They also found that father's occupation was not consistently related to children's achievement. Desai (1979) observed no relationship between socio- economic status and achievement.

Socio-economic variables related students determined selection but were not relevant to subsequent academic performance (Nagpal, 1979).

Menon (1972) found that job aspiration, educational aspiration and general ambition were strongly associated with high achievement, particularly in girls.

There are a few typical cases of equal importance. sear (1940) observed that children with a past history of success showed very little variability in aspiration. Most of them maintained the typical small positive goal discrepancy. Children with past history of failure showed a much higher goal discrepancy and variability. Some had very high positive goals discrepancies, they set their level of aspiration very much above their immediate past performance. Similar patterns of aspiration have been observed in later clinical studies the level of aspiration.

Studies of Gould and Kaplan (1940), Sears (1940), Holt (1942), Schultz and Ricciuti (1954) found no relationship between scholastic achievement and level of aspiration. Sharma (1979) also found that the level of aspiration did not influence academic achievement.

Muthayya (1962) concluded that high achievers and low achievers in scholastic do not significantly differ in aspiration level. Radha (1985) found that the level of aspiration has not been found to have significant bearing on academic achievement.

Gates and Jersild (1948) have stated that the level of aspiration is closely related to success and failure in college and that it may represent a goal or desire to improve the performance. Lowel that and Atkinson (1953) reported a positive but low and not significant relationship between the level of aspiration and the achievement motive among high and how achievers.

Kuppuswamy (1974) informed that the achievement in school is closely related to the level of aspiration. Shukla (1973) observed that the level of aspiration determines the limits of academic achievement to some extent. Hussain (1977) concluded that the academic performance of the group showing moderate goal discrepancy was better than that of the groups showing either high or low goal discrepancy, implying a curvilinear relationship between the level of aspiration and academic performance.

Bryan and Locke (1967) concluded that academic performance can be increased by suggesting what level a person should aspire for. Sears (1940) and Rotter (1943) have found that groups with a history of poor academic achievement had higher average goal discrepancy scores than groups with a history of high achievement.

Ramkumar (1972) observed a strong association between achievement and goal discrepancy and pointed out that achievement is higher with a decline in goal discrepancy scores.

Several investigators are of the opinion that academic adjustment or adjustment to college is an important factor in academic achievement. Students in general and under-achievers in particular have frequently reported problems of adjustment in college. Carson (1927) observed that on entering the college and freshman faces a number of new adjustment problems for which he is usually unprepared. Hence, Stogdill (1929), Angel (1930) and Philips (1930) emphasized the responsibility of the college to help in solving student's problems. Nagpal (1979) stating that the academic adjustment of undergraduate engineering students was an important correlate of over- and under-achievement.

Abraham (1974) revealed that the achievement level was associated with personal adjustments and social adjustment. Goswami (1978) reports that global self-concept and scholastic achievement had s significant positive correlation.

Reddy (1974) found academic adjustment significantly related to the scholastic performance of secondary schools pupils. soman (1977) also observed that personal adjustment variables had a considerable influence on achievement. Vashishtha (1991) found a positive relationship between adjustment and achievement.

In Salunke's (1979) study it was observed that educational facilities and emotional happiness in the home contributed positively to the academic achievement. Saun (1980) observed a significant difference between the high and the low achieving females in health, social, emotional and educational areas of adjustment.

Steinzer (1944), Cattell (1945) and Thompson (1948) pointed out that over-achievers were characterized by good adjustment to school and greater awareness and responsiveness to environmental influence. Frankel (1960) found that over-achievers conforming to school regulations adjusted better to the academic situation. Christenson (1956), Popham and Moore (1960) and Roberts (1962) observed that over-achievers differed significantly from under-achievers differed significantly from under-achievers in their adjustment to college. French (1958) considers that lack of adjustment to college life in the freshman introduces extraneous influences on scholastic success.

Berger and Sutker (1956) observed that students with adequate personality adjustment achieved better in academic performance. Brown (1953), Wellington (1965) and Graff (1957) demonstrated that high-achievers tend to be more stable and adjusted than low-achievers. Scott (1958) felt that only the best mode of adjustment maximizes the chance of success.

Soman's (1977) study revealed that the dominant personality factor identified for the over-achievers was individual adjustment factor. Dhami (1974) concluded that there was a higher relationship between scholastic achievement and emotional stability in the case of 9th class boys than in the case of 10th class boys who were more anxiety-ridden due to the coming public examinations. George (1966) mentioned that the pupils of 10th class with high intelligence were identified as better adjusted and higher achievers. Goswami (1978) found that scholastic achievement is highly correlated with the concept of adjustment.

Congdon (1943), Huston and Marzolf (1944), Hibler and Larson (1944) and Caroll and Jones (1944) have found several adjustment problems associated with under-achievement. Johnson (1947) held that poor performance in college was due to unsatisfactory adjustment in college. Anderson (1951) observed that many under-achievers were not beset with serious personal problems. Wig and Nagpal (1972) found that the failure group had poor adjustment at school and college but not at university.

Assum and levy (1947) found personal adjustment positively related to scholastic achievement. Even when the typically maladjusted student was above his more fortunate fellow student, intellectually he often fell below the normal achievement. Stagmen (1953) found that unstable and maladjusted students had done less well than their stable contemporaries.

Martin (1952) held personal maladjustment bordering on neuroticism as characteristic feature of failing students. Jenson (1958) reported a general tendency for non-achievers to encounter more adjustment problems.

Abraham (1974) observed that group adjustment, socio-personal adjustment were found to be the factors responsible for explaining total variance in the case of under-achievers.

Bhagirath (1979) found that the teachers and the students perceived the correlates of academic achievement as intelligence, character, creativity, punctuality, activeness, alertness, efficiency, educational adjustment, school and social adjustment, social/emotional adjustment and intelligence/social adjustment.

Rani (1980) and Shasidhar (1981) concluded that the academic achievement was influenced by institutional factors with the sample of schedule caste students.

Reddy (1981) studied the interrelationship between organizational climate, socio-economic status, students' perception of rewarding behaviour and the academic achievement of a random stratified sample of 1607 pupils from 103 schools of Telangana area in A.P. and concluded that academic achievement level of schools having the organizational climate profile of (i) controlled, (ii) controlled -cum-paternal-cum-closed, (iii) controlled-cum-autonomous, and (iv) controlled-cum-open to be 305.34, 303.47, 325.73 and 364.54 respectively out of a total of 600 marks.

Desai (1979) and Hirunval (1980) observed a positive relationship between classroom climate and pupils' academic achievement in their studies conducted in Gujarat. Pal (1982) identified that good schooling, interest and industriousness played an important role in the learning of science. He also concluded that students belonging to the advanced schools had done better in science achievement test than those in less-advanced schools having the same or more or less identical general ability.

Subramanyam's (1981) study highlighted the importance of conditions at school vis-a-vis pupils' achievement. Multiple regression analysis of the data showed that personal characteristics of the children contributed to a large extent to their reading achievement and between the two factors, namely, school condition and home condition, and an increase in school condition was likely to lead to better achievement. In another study made by Srinivasa Rao and Subramanyam (1982) it was revealed that among the school factors, accommodation, educational level and experience of teachers, availability of instructional material, books and reading room facilities influenced the reading attainment of children positively.

Another study on classroom climate conducted in Rajasthan with a sample of 1294 by Verma (1977) concludes as ; the rural school classes showed slight superiority over the urban school classes as far as acceptance, trustfulness, adaptability and emotional relationship dimensions of the classroom climate were concerned; the academic achievements of the urban and rural schools were at par but there was significant difference in the intellectual standards of the rural and the urban pupils; the mean differences of the classroom climate for adaptability and emotional relationship were significant in favour of the classrooms of the private schools; the classes of the privately managed schools have a more learning-conducive climate; the socio-emotional climate of the classroom not only predicted and influenced the pupil's academic achievement but also affected his classroom behavioral development; the classroom climate was positively correlated with the studiousness factor of the sociometric test; the classroom climate was negatively correlated with the behavioral development of the pupils in the class and also with the mischievousness factor; the pupils, classroom behavior was positively correlated with their academic achievement. All the components of the studiousness factor and the composite studiousness factor were positively correlated and the mischievousness factor and its components were negatively correlated with the pupils' academic achievement.

Educational opportunities, though open to all, do not seem to engage to any reasonable extent the capacities of those who seek to avail them of. An eternal question baffling parents, educators and national planners is : why do students of demonstrated ability flop in their academic efforts at school or college examinations? Academic under-achievement, more than academic failure, constitutes a grave problem as it amounts to wastage of human resources which is construed as an irreparable loss to the society, which, a developing country like ours, can ill afford. This stimulated a number of researchers to undertake studies, like the present study, on factors influencing achievements, a review of which is presented here under.

The concepts of over-achievement and under-achievement, logically speaking, are meaningful in relation to some expected level of performance. Theoretically, if one's performance is superior to the expected standard of performance then one may be regarded as over-achiever, whereas when one's performance is inferior then one may be regarded as under-achiever.

Scientists like Stanley, Ross, Frumar and Frazen feel that the phenomenon of over-achievement is, logically, spurious and meaningless since, according to them, no one can operate above the level of one's potential ability, from which most often, the standard of expected performance is derived. However, they assert that under-achievement is the indication level of full expression of one's potential ability. On accepting the theoretical definition of the concept of under-achievement which stresses that under-achievement is meaningful in relation to one's actual performance that may be adjudged, we are justified to ask as to from which level the expected performance comes.

Broadly speaking, there are two ways open for answering the question regarding the standard of expected performance. Either, the standard of expected performance may be subjective, or it may be objective. The subjective standard of expected performance may further be classified into two categories. In one type of the subjective standard of expected performance, the individual himself determines the standard of performance; whereas in the second type of subjective standard, the expected standard of performance is stipulated by the person who is operating as a 'significant-other' (parent or teacher) in one's process of socialization. We all know that the subjective standards of performance determined by significant others are so much subjective and irrational that they are rarely attainable. How-so-ever hard a student may try it is not possible to satisfy one's parents or teachers through his achievement.

Psychologically speaking, the subjective standard of expected performance, irrespective of the fact, whether it is arising from within or it is imposed by the parents or teachers from outside, is representing man's hopes and aspirations which are endless.

One more type of the subjective standard of expected performance is representing aspirations and hopes of one's spiritual leader or hero. Such a standard of expected performance is most often unrealizable and may be termed as the ideal standard of expected performance.

The expected standard of performance which comes from within the individual, is the outcome of his own aspirations and satisfactions related to his achievements. Previous experiences of success result in guiding a person for raising his level of expectation. Some individuals may be satisfied with the previous achievement while others may want to settle for higher grades. They are often eager to learn more, confident to do it and ambitious to achieve more.

Research Design

Research design decides the fate of any research proposal and its outcome. As such it is regarded as the heart of any research. Designing provides a picture for the whole study before it. It is, in a simple language, a plan of action, It is, therefore, desirable to have a methodically designed research plan. So the following aspects of the research design have been discussed in detail.

The operational definitions of the different terms used, the various hypotheses that were framed for verification in the present study and the rationale of these hypotheses have been discussed.

The sampling techniques selected, the reasons for selection of a particular sampling technique, and the selection of sample according to different variables have also been discussed in detail.

The selection of suitable tool for collection of data, and the procedure followed in administering the tool to collecting the data required for the present study have also been explained.

Before going into the details of the sample, sampling techniques, variables and hypotheses, it is worthwhile to discuss the operational definitions of the key terms used in the present study which will enlighten the characteristics involved in each term.

Operational Definitions

The operational definitions of the important terms used in the present study are discussed and defined herewith.

Achievement

Achievement in an educational institution may be taken to mean any desirable learning that is observed in the student. Since the word desirable implies a value judgement, it is obvious that a particular learning may be referred to as achievement or otherwise depending on whether it is considered desirable or not. Understood in this way, any behaviour that is learned may come within the scope of achievement. Achievement, according to Smith (1969), and Spencer and HELMRICH (1983), is the task oriented behaviour that allows the individual's performance to be evaluated according to some internally or externally imposed criterion, that involves the individual in competing with others, or that otherwise involves some standard of excellence (Morgan, et al., 1986).

There is no gainsaying the fact that learning is not limited to mere acquisition of information, it also includes attitudes, interests, values, etc. Modern personality characteristics of the individual are learned. Therefore, the acquisition of desirable characteristics is as much an achievement as is knowledge of the principles of science or facts, world history or language and literature. Although achievement is used in this broad sense it is customary for schools and colleges to be concerned to a great extent with the development of knowledge, understanding and acquisition of skills (Naryana Rao, 1980). This may be in part owing to the fact that in the intellectual field the teacher can be relatively more certain of achieving the objectives he had set for himself than in other areas or domains.

The teacher or the institution has certain objectives which are often stated as the development of desirable characteristics of personality. Though this is undoubtedly a worthy goal, it is doubtful whether anything beyond the most superficial change could be obtained with the small number of hours contact between the teacher and the taught in the college. Thus in practice, the objectives are necessarily restricted to the imparting of various types of subject-matter knowledge.

Academic achievement is related to the acquisition of principles and generalizations and the capacity to perform efficiently, certain manipulations of objects, symbols and ideas. Assessment of academic performance has been largely conformed to the evaluation in terms of information, knowledge and understanding. It is universally accepted that the acquisition of factual data is not an end in itself but an individual who has received education should show evidence of having understood them. But, for obvious reasons, the examinations are largely confined to the measurement of the amount of information which students have acquired.

Wood and Learned (1938) concluded from their well known Pennsylvania study that education was unavoidably intellectual in which knowledge was the dominating feature of educational outcomes. It is perhaps the only accepted basis of promotion or fulfillment of requirements for degree or diploma. It is the actual or assumed possession of knowledge that counts for admission into a class or course. Educational measurements may be made with reference to either the aims or the results of education or both. The acquisition of knowledge consists of the registering of data or the making of a datum either more definite and indelible or meaningful. This conception of acquiring knowledge assumes that the student is an active organism in a stimulus-response situation, that the student interprets his experience, that he shows evidence of having registered and interpreted the datum by his appropriate response to it and that in future situations he will be guided by prior experience. Understood in this way measurement can be in terms of subject matter and this does not claim to minimize the importance of the other aspects of education.

Examinations in one form or another were employed by people ever since the days of early civilizations. Paul F. Cressey, a sociologist, attributes the remarkable stability of the old Chinese civilization among other things to her highly organized examination system. Examinations are not only used extensively, they vitally affect and determine the careers of students. From the earliest time teachers have examined as well as taught. Some kind of measurement or evaluation seems suitable in education and it is an essential part of the teaching, learning process.

Achievement in terms of subject matter is conventionally assessed in our institutions by employing a system of marks or grades. It has been strongly argued that marks are necessary for effective teaching, learning. Trabue (1926) felt that, for classification, guidance and evidence of effort, marks are necessary. A committee of Principals of California listed the purposes of marks as the indication of the degree of mastery of subject matter and the prediction of future success. Madsen (1930) points out that marks set goals and motivate the students. Symonds (1927) listed among the purposes of marks, incitement of study, promotion of competition, determination of promotion, assistance in education and vocational guidance, awarding credits and honors. It is universally accepted that marks serve as the basis of classification and certification, motivation and measurement of educational performance.

Science

Science has helped the man to acquire supremacy over nature. It has greatly affected the way the people view themselves and the world around them. The wonderful achievements of science have glorified the modern world and illuminated the human creative potential.

In ancient times, most of the people believed that natural events and everything that happens to them are because of the actions of the God and Spirits. But the ancient Greeks were among the first to use systematic observation and reasoning to analyse natural happenings. As scientific thinking gradually developed, nature has seen less and less as the product of mysterious spiritual forces. Moreover, people began to feel that nature could be understood and even controlled through science.

Science, in literal sense, means 'the pursuit of knowledge'. The word 'Science' comes from the Latin word 'Scientia'. which means 'knowledge'. The term science in the sense of knowledge was used for long to include the entire subject matter of study. Though it is correct, it does not imply that, all knowledge is science. This is very clear by the fact that all the branches of social sciences and humanities are universally excluded from the preview of sciences. The reason offered for this is that the conclusions in social sciences and humanities are beyond verification and quantification. The post war efforts by various people to elevate the status of humanities and social sciences to science, proved to be a futile effort. Again the reason was the inability to measure, quantify and verify the human mind and behaviour. Thus, the facility to measure, quantify and verify the object in question is the part of science. Its conclusions are universal. The body of knowledge is factual and verifiable, and the results are data-based.

Science is usually defined as a systematized knowledge. It is not a casual heap of disconnected scraps, but the bonds of union and the principles of arrangement is knowledge and it is mainly practical and social.

The knowledge is ordered, but it is not ordered from the stand point of and for the sake of knowledge. Not, thus, the presence of a peculiar principle and method of systematizing. Science is the knowledge that is systematized from the stand point of and for the sake of knowledge as distinct from the stand point of practice and social intercourse. specifically, this means that the subject matter of knowledge is selected, formulated and arranged, with special reference to the exhibition of relations of intellectual dependence which its various parts sustain one another.

Many efforts, hence, were made to arrive at a precise meaning and definition of the word science by avoiding the loopholes. Let us see some of the important definition to understand the science.

The Columbia Encyclopedia defined science as ..... accumulated and systematized learning, in general usage, restricted to natural phenomenon. The progress of science is marked not only by an accumulation of facts, but by the emergence of scientific method and of the scientific attitude.

According to Frederic Fitzpatrick, "Science is cumulative and endless series of empirical observations which result in the formation of concepts and theories, with both concepts and theories being subject to modification in the light of further empirical observations. Science is both a body of knowledge and a process of acquiring it."

Albert Einstein felt that "Science searches for relations, which are thought to exist independently of the searching individual". whitehead, the famous philosopher, defines science as "an attempt to systematize our knowledge of the circumstances in which recognitions occur". Ames, M.V. says, "Science is more than a compilation of facts. It is a method of thinking and working, a way of solving problems". Conant (1948) defines that, "science is an interconnected series of concepts and theories. Science is a body of knowledge and the process of acquiring and refining knowledge."

Hurd opined that "facts themselves do not make a science. Science is not simply an abstraction from empirical data, but an intellectual occasion often suggested by data, it is the discerning of order among the data that makes the science. Science is an intellectual activity which arises from personal experience and takes place in the minds of men. It is simply a way of using human intelligence to achieve a better understanding of nature and nature's laws".

B.F. Skinner, a great psychologist, defined science as "First of all, science is a set of attitudes. It is a disposition to deal with facts rather than with what some one has said about them". Green, A.W. says "Science is a way of investigation". In the words of Poincare, "Science is built of facts as a house is built of stones, but an accumulation of facts is no more a science than a heap of stones". According to Weinbeg and Shabat "Science is certain way of looking at the world".

Since life in the present world invariably warrants, to variable degrees, knowledge of scientific facts and laws, science has now become everyday science for every body. Teaching of everyday science for everybody has become an unavoidable part of general education. Science takes its place side by side with other subjects as an essential element of one's education. It affords a knowledge of certain facts and laws and an insight into methods and dates peculiar to the domain of science.

The teaching of science like any other subject of school stage can be justified for various reasons. The very nature of the subject justifies its inclusion in the school curriculum. science prepares pupils to think and sharpen their intellect making them more careful and systematic in reasoning. It provides unique training in truth, inculcates a spirit of inquiry, develops the capacity to know the unknown and gives strength to face failures.

The report of the education commission (1964-66) laid much emphasis on science- based education. In its own words, "There is, one thing about which we feel with no doubt or hesitation, that is, science-based education in coherence with Indian culture and values can alone provide the foundation as also the instrument for the nation's progress, security and welfare".

In its recommendations on "education and productivity", the commission further mentions that "Science education should become on integral part of school education, and ultimately some study of science should become a part of all courses in the humanities and social sciences".

Science education in daily life, specially at the school stage, is necessary for several reasons. Firstly, the rapid growth of science and technology is influencing almost all walks of life. In fact, this rapid growth is resulting in the production of altogether new materials, new uses of old materials as well as providing the society with powerful tools capable of bringing about changes in the environment. Secondly, significant portions of the students terminate their studies after primary education and therefore there is an imperative need to provide them education, informally or non-formally, on continuing basis about the ongoing developments in the areas of science and technology having direct relevance to life. Thirdly, in view of the nature of science, the scientific laws and principles being generalization of common experiences, the need for relating science with the life of community becomes quite obvious. A comparison between the processes of science and those used in agriculture, health and hygiene revealing the similarity between them also endorses the some view. Lastly. Only the important objectives of education will bring about desired behavioural change. If science is taught in isolation, as a body of facts and principles alone, it can hardly meet the above objectives. It is therefore, all the more, necessary to make deliberate efforts to dovetial science education with life.

Science can be conveniently divided into two branches. Viz., 1. Physical sciences-which concern with non-living objects, and 2. Biological or life sciences-which concern with living organisms.

Achievement Test

The term achievement is often understood in terms of a student's scores in a certain test. If, for instance, a student is tested in two school subjects, say English and Mathematics and in one subject he gets 50% marks while in other 70% marks, it is understood that his achievement in English in which he gets 50% marks is not better than that in mathematics in which he gets 70% marks. This is loose way of understanding the concept of achievement. More intelligently understood, achievement means one's learning attainments, accomplishments, proficiencies, etc. Achievement is directly related to a pupil's growth and development in educational situations where learning and teaching are intended to go on simultaneously. Achievement involves aptitude for learning, readiness for learning and opportunity for learning (Bhatia, 1991). Besides these factors, it also involves health and physical fitness, motivation, special aptitude, and emotional balance.

Freeman (1965) defines a test of educational achievement as a test designed to measure knowledge, understanding, skills in a specified subject or group of subject. Thus according to him, an educational achievement test measures an individual's knowledge and understanding or skills in a particular branch of knowledge. Further, freeman is of the view that through educational achievement test, it is possible to ascertain how much does a person know after receiving education or training in a particular branch of knowledge. Standardized achievement tests are used to determine the degree of achievement in a specific subject matter (Smith, Krouse and Atkinson, 1969). Achievement tests (Best, 1982) attempt to measure what an individual has learned - his or her present level of performance.

Anastasi (1968) has discussed that various uses of achievement test- achievement tests are used to ascertain the attainment of minimum performance standards. In other words, an achievement test is to find out whether an individual has attained the required ability in a given field of knowledge or activity. Another important use of an achievement test is to be seen when there is a need for selecting candidates in regard to certain jobs or courses.

An achievement test is also used for purposes of guidance and counselling. It has been found useful in remedial teaching programs as well as in determining the class to which a student should be admitted into. Administration of these tests at regular intervals is helpful to the teachers in knowing the kinds of difficulties faced by the students in learning. Finally it may be stated that the achievement test may be used as an aid in the evaluation of teaching, the importance of instructional techniques, and the revision of curriculum content.

Residential Junior Colleges

In the residential junior colleges, students stay on in the college campus with their teachers instead of coming daily from their houses. So they spend all their time either on the college premises or in the hostels, and pursue studies under the constant supervision of teachers. Such colleges of Intermediate or +2 level are considered residential junior colleges.

Non-residential Junior Colleges

The students of these colleges are in the college campus only during instructional hours and spend their remaining time at home or at other places. Such colleges are considered non-residential junior colleges.

Private Junior Colleges

The junior colleges managed by private organizations or persons, either partially or totally, were included in private junior colleges. The government recognized junior colleges and government aided junior colleges were also included under private junior colleges.

Government Junior Colleges

The junior colleges under the sole management of government officials were included in this category. So the colleges managed by the government of Andhra Pradesh and the Andhra Pradesh Residential Junior Colleges' Society established by the Government of Andhra Pradesh were included in this category.

Variables

Variables are a necessary requisite for any worthwhile research for the purpose of comparison. For the present study the following variables are considered. They are: residential versus non-residential, private versus government, and boys versus girls. The rationale for choosing the above stated variables is discussed herewith.

Residential* versus *Non-Residential Junior Colleges

Education has become indispensable for every one. The machinery of government is inadequate to educate all. According to earlier targets, we had to educate all children by the time they attain 14 years of age. The year 1960 was thought of as the year for fulfilling the target. Even though three decades have elapsed since then we managed to educate nearly half to our population, Here, one must not forget that private schools and colleges have the lion's share in promoting education.

On the old Indian educational scenario, the gurukulas (residential places of learning) played a very prominent role in educating the pupils or disciples. Later on, this system failed to cope up with the changes that occurred in the society and disappeared almost, to say frankly, and a new set-up of educational institutions came into existence and took deep roots. With the new system introduced and implemented by the British, many people got educated and obtained proficiency and efficiency in many fields of education and vocation.

Though the formal system of educational set-up has been providing education at its best to its non-boarders, it has certain disadvantages, which include - poor teacher taught relationship, improper discipline, under achievement, irrelevant teaching and etc. At this hour, the importance of residential system offered by the 'gurukulas' in good olden days is identified as the best system to solve many problems in educating a child and to provide quality education through better teaching and learning strategies. This thought gave rise to many residential schools and colleges. The residential schools- such as Andhra Pradesh Residential Schools, Andhra Pradesh social Welfare Residential Schools, Jawahar Navodays Schools, Central Schools, and Colleges- such as Andhra Pradesh Residential Junior Colleges, Andhra Pradesh Residential Degree Colleges, etc., have been established by both the state government and the central government. The residential institutions in Andhra Pradesh have excelled in academic achievement and allied areas and proved worthy.

On seeing the performance of the students of A.P. Residential junior colleges established in Andhra Pradesh in the early 1980s by the Government of Andhra Pradesh, the private managements started establishing residential junior colleges, and at present they outnumber the non-residential colleges—both government and private—in volume and strength.

Establishment of residential junior colleges in private sector, that too without any permission from the government, is not an amazing thing, but these private residential junior colleges are flourishing by leaps and bounds. For this the reasons are many and multidimensional. Let as discuss in detail the merits and limitations of both non-residential and residential junior colleges.

The Government of Andhra Pradesh has been spending to the tune of Rs. 200 crores on Intermediate education. The results are not in proportion to the expenditure incurred. Only 40 per cent of the students pass. In other words, two thirds of its expenditure is squandered away for nothing (Rathaiah and Bhaskara Rao, 1990). When private educational institution are compared with those run by the government, the former are far better than the latter in respect of physical facilities, administration and staff. Above all they excel government colleges, in the matter of results.

Now private residential colleges have come up. They have been welcomed by those who want admission into professional colleges. in fact they have been weaning away a large number of students from government colleges. The government institutions and government aided private colleges have been unable to attract the cream of intermediate students. What are the features of private residential system that have been attractive to students? Several questions arise when we discuss the problem in detail (Bhaskara Rao, 1989).

Is the failure of private aided and government colleges a factor in the success of private residential college system ? Is the quality of teaching superior in private residential colleges to that of government and aided colleges? Whether laboratory ,library and other necessary physical facilities contribute to their success? Is it the main aim of private residential system to earn more and more money? Are these colleges getting good results because of malpractices? Is there any real need for this rapid growth of residential colleges? Are these colleges a burden to the government or to the society?

Many think that the fast expansion of private colleges reflect the failure of the government in providing educational facilities to its people. But the reality is that education should not be monopolized by the government. Such monopoly involves colossal financial expenditure which is to proportionately matched by results. Even in the most advanced countries government will not undertake the entire responsibility of educating its public. Except in the socialist countries, government does not undertake the total responsibility of education.

When the private residential colleges grow, a large number of people who can afford to spend on education opt for these private residential colleges and those who cannot go the government institutions. With this the government can disburden itself, for, most of the financially sound students get their education without compelling the government to spend anything on them. Then, there will be a healthy competition between the two. So privatization of education brings healthy competition between the government and the private colleges, reduces the pressure on government institutions and offers chances to the students who can afford to have such education.

Time is precious and the two years a student spends in his intermediate course is more precious than any other period because that decides his future fate (Rathaiah and Bhaskara Rao 1990). In non-residential government and aided colleges, teachers and students stay together for only five to six hours a day. The rest of the 18 to 19 hours the student is left to his free will. Even if he wishes to clear his doubts, teachers are not available. With the result, the influence of the society is greater on him than on his counterpart in residential colleges.

A student, on the other hand, is given ample opportunity in residential colleges to pursue his education with single minded devotion and undivided attention, as the teachers are available at hand to clear his doubts. As the calibre of the students is very high, the teachers are always on the alert. As both teachers and students are committed to a goal and are led on the track of well-organized schedules there is no room for diversion either for the student or for the teacher. This is evident from the wonderful results they produce. Unprecedented rush to these private residential colleges is an illustrative proof of their good performance. The colleges speak for themselves by their results.

In respect of facilities—buildings, hostels, laboratories, play fields—the private residential colleges score points against the government managed or aided colleges. Teaching, learning, playing and extra-curricular activities are all in a single campus. They are not touched by the ripples and waves of academic restlessness of other colleges. They are the real, isolated islands of learning.

Students at the Intermediate level pass through adolescence (Bhaskara Rao, 1989). They need careful handling as they pass through physiological changes with their attendant problems. The big question is who will devote time and energy to their problems. Parents and the society are too bust to spare time for them. The teachers of government managed or aided colleges are deeply absorbed with their organizational problems. They are more often than not pegged down with their grievances. They, hence or otherwise, do not undertake the responsibility of the students.

The residential colleges are started for this specific purpose of attending to the needs of Intermediate students. As the teachers, students and authorities are under one roof any problem can be easily solved giving no room for dissatisfaction. These colleges forge emotional integration also among the students.

These residential colleges have been attracting students from all over the State. So the students are given a wonderful opportunity to mingle and develop their personalities (Rathaiah and Bhaskara

Rao, 1990), While other colleges are the victims of local and non-local restraints, these residential colleges fully represent the culture of the state.

Finally, the residential system or the old gurukula system which we gave up long ago has come to say. Residential colleges, may overcome the maladies that afflict the academic world to a certain extent.

Considering the above facts, the students of residential and non-residential junior colleges were taken into consideration to study the achievement in science.

Private versus *Government Junior Colleges*

The reputation of private junior colleges is generally far superior when compared with that of the government junior colleges. In private junior colleges the students are exposed to better conditions and better study atmosphere. The laboratories and libraries will be better. If better facilities are not provided in private colleges, the parents will question the authorities concerned as they pay higher fees for their children.

The quality of teaching is also supposed to be better in private junior colleges. The lecturers take more interest in teaching in private colleges as they are always or to some extent in the fear of either losing their jobs or immediately being questioned by the management about the quality of their teaching.

Since the standard of teaching is supposed to be different in private and government junior colleges, the science achievement of the students will be different and hence this variable is taken into consideration for this study.

Boys versus *Girls*

In olden days, boys were educated and the girls were restricted to their kitchens by their adult community. Times changed and the adults recognized the importance of women's education. In the words of our late Prime Minister Pandit Jawaharlal Nehru, 'if you educate a man you educate only one person' if you educate woman you educate the entire family'. In due course, women's education gained importance and many parents are encouraging their daughters to pursue higher education. Women are also showing excellence in all fields and their presence is felt almost in all fields.

As the physiological conditions, exposure to society, education and other aspects of girls and boys vary differently, there may be a significant difference in the performance. The boys may be exposed to the society to a larger extent, but the girls spend most of their time in going through books or helping their parents at home. These factors will show their influence on their mental development and performance.

It is especially important to study the level of achievement because they just enter the adolescent stage, which is otherwise known as the period of stress and strain. At this stage, this sample finds that they find it extremely difficult to adjust themselves in the society because they are accepted neither as adults nor as children. It is also familiar that girls mature faster than boys at the early adolescent stage, both physically and mentally. The above factors will have their own impact on the achievement. so, a comparison between boys and girls will reveal the differences existing in achievement.

Hypotheses

Achievement is a paramount importance, particularly in the present socio-economic and cultural contexts, and great emphasis is placed on achievement right from the beginning of the formal education. It is a task-oriented behaviour that allows the individual's performance to be evaluated according to some internally or externally imposed criterion, that involves some standard of excellence.

Achievement is related to the acquisition of principles and generalizations and the capacity to perform efficiently, certain manipulations of objects, symbols and ideas. Assessment of achievement has been largely conformed to the evaluation in terms of knowledge and understanding. It is universally accepted that the acquisition of factual data is not an end in itself but that an individual who has received education should show the evidence of having understood them. But, for obvious reasons the examinations are largely confined to the measurement of the amount of information acquired by students.

Achievement in terms of subject matter is conventionally assessed in our institutions by employing a system of marks or grades, and it has been strongly argued that marks are necessary for effective teaching learning. Marks also set goals and motivate the students. It is universally accepted that marked serve as the basis of classification and certification, measurement and analysis of educational achievement.

The students studying in residential junior colleges stay round the clock in college campus and they will be under a strict vigilance of the wardens and lecturers. The students go through the lessons regularly and get their doubts clarified. The resident lecturers also check the students's performance regularly. And at the same time these colleges will have well-equipped laboratories, libraries and other centres of learning.

Contrary to this, the students studying in non-residential colleges will be in the college for about 5 or 6 hours a day and the balance of the time will be spent according to their interest. As there will be no watch on their studies, these students do not try to study regularly and get their doubts clarified on the spot.

As stated earlier, the variables, namely, residential versus non-residential junior college students, private versus government junior college students and boys versus girls were considered.

The following were the hypotheses formulated.

Hypothesis 1

The Intermediate students will possess high achievement in science.

Hypothesis 2

there will be a significant difference in the level of achievement of the students of residential and non-residential junior colleges.

Hypothesis 3

There will be a significant difference in the achievement of the students of private and government junior colleges

Hypothesis 4

There will be a significant difference in the achievement of boys and girls of junior colleges.

Sample

After finalizing the variables of the present study, consideration was given to whether the entire population is to be made the subject for data collection or a particular group is to be selected as representative of the whole population. The 'entire population' here refers to all the senior Intermediate students of Andhra Pradesh.

Selection of a group as a representative of the entire population was found to be more convenient and suitable. This techniques leads to a considerable saving of time, effort and finance. The number of students selected is small, and so it is possible to make a detailed and intensive study. This generally leads to more accurate and reliable results. As this sampling technique has many advantages, it was selected for the collection of data.

In any social research, various methods are utilized for selection and drawing of samples. After a detailed study of all these methods, and considering the variables selected for the research work, the stratified sampling method was found most suitable. In the stratified sampling method, the entire population is divided into smaller homogeneous groups (Best) or strata, an then the sample is selected within each group. Every sampling unit in the population is placed in one of the strata prior to the selection of the sample so that the sum of the strata is identical with the population. Stratified sampling method has certain merits and advantages as a techniques of sampling. Auckoff has rightly said that 'stratified sampling enables the researcher to make a comparison of properties of the strata as well as to estimate population characteristics (Kerlinger, 1964).

The investigators, in the stratified sampling method, have greater control over the selection of the sample when compared with random sampling. In random sampling, although every group has a chance of being selected and included in the sample, there is every possibility, and sometimes it does happen, that certain important groups are left unrepresented. But in stratified sampling method no important group is likely to be left out.

Stratified sampling method is the ideal one when comparison between different variables has to be made. For example, if comparison has to be made between residential and non-residential junior college students, it would be very difficult to select the required number of units through any other method of sampling. If any other method is used, the problem of bias and prejudice creeps in.

Replacement of units is also possible in the stratified sampling method. Normally if a particular unit is not accessible to a study, it is difficult to replace it by another, but in this method it is possible. Stephen states that 'stratification automatically brings about a replacement of persons lost to the sample, by persons of the same stratum, thus partly correcting the basis that would result if there were no replacements of losses (Festinger and Daniel, 1976). As the entire population is divided into particular strata it is easy and connivent to replace an inaccessible case by an accessible one.

In this stratified sampling method, much depends on the stratification process. The following precautions were taken while stratifying the population: the variables involved in the study were taken note of; care was taken to see that each stratum in the universe was large enough in size so that selection of items could be made on random basis; the strata formed were definite and clear cut; each stratum was free from the influence of the other; that there was no overlapping.

Before actually selecting the sample, certain fundamental principles were considered to make the sample scientific and clear-out.

Firstly, the 'universe' is to be clearly defined. In the technical phraseology of research, the whole population out of which the samples are selected is known as the 'universe'. For the present research work, the universe includes all the students of senior Intermediate studying in residential and non-residential junior colleges of Andhra Pradesh. But, the study was limited to a particular geographical area to facilitate appropriate sample selection and to avoid basis an prejudice.

Secondly, a decision has to be made about the units of the sample. A unit of sample may be a house, a family, a group of individuals or a single individual. A good unit should possess the following characteristics—

(A) Clarity: The unit should be clearly defined in unambiguous terms. This would make the study easy and efficient. For the present research work, a sampling unit was defined as a pupil of senior Intermediate studying in any college in Andhra Pradesh;

(B) Suitability: A good unit should be well suited to the problem under study. Since the problem is related to the achievement of residential and non-residential senior Intermediate students, the unit selected is well suited to the problem;

(C) *Assessibility:* The unit selected should be easily accessible to the researchers. If the units selected are difficult to reach and if the researchers fail to make use of them, the study would be vitiated. The selected sampling unit, *i.e.*, a senior Intermediate student is easily accessible since the researchers could be approached in any junior college.

Thirdly, it is looked upon the availability or preparation of the source list. This is an important factor that makes the representative selection possible. A source list is the list which contains the names of the units of the universe from which the sample may be selected. It may exist even before the beginning of the project or it may be prepared afresh by the investigators. Without a source list, study through the sampling method is not possible. For the present research work, a source list, consisting of the names of residential junior colleges and non-residential junior colleges of Andhra Pradesh, was used. Care was taken to see that the source list was up-to-date and valid and that there was no repetition of the names of colleges. This source list was found to be relevant and suitable because it includes the colleges as the study deals with the senior Intermediate students.

Besides considering these principles, it is extremely important to think about the size of the sample to be selected. If the sample is either very small or very large, it will make the study, difficult and will also make the results untenable. According to Parten 'an optimum sample in survey is the one which fulfils the requirements of effective representativeness, reliability and flexibility. The sample should be small enough to avoid intolerable sampling error'. The size of the sample for the present research work was decided after considering the following factors.

Since an intensive study was planned, a very large number of samples were not selected. In case of an intensive study, very large number of samples were not so useful as they involve huge consumption of the resources. A small sample was found to be convenient.

The size and selection of the samples are also influenced by the nature of the universe. If the universe is homogeneous, even a small-sized sample may yield dependable and required results. If the universe is heterogeneous, small-sized samples may not be useful. In case of the present study, the homogenous universe was split into smaller homogeneous groups and the samples were selected from these groups. For example, all the senior intermediate students were broadly grouped under residential and non-residential students. A sample was selected from each of these two groups.

The investigators need to determine the number of the groups to be formed. In case the number of groups proposed is large, the size of the samples shall have to be large so that every group should be of proper size and suit the requirements of the study. In case the number of groups proposed is small, even small-sized samples can fulfil the requirement. In the case of the present study, the number of groups into which the universe was divided are - girls and boys, private and government junior colleges and residential and non-residential junior colleges. Since the number of groups is more, a reasonable large sample was selected from each of these groups.

Practical considerations and accuracy also play a vital role in determining the size of the sample. Every study is guided by certain practical considerations such as time, resources, accessibility of data, etc. Usually, it is believed that a large sized sample is more representative and generally produces accurate results. This, of course, depends upon the technique of sampling used. If the techniques is scientific, even small-sized samples can produce dependable and accurate results. While selecting the size of the sample for the present study, practical considerations like the availability of resources and time were taken into consideration. Care was taken to make the sample selection technique as scientific as possible.

The size of the sample is also governed by the size of the tools to be used. In case the tools are short, and the questions asked pertain to certain limited factors, a large sample can be selected. In case the tools are large and the questions complicated, the sample should be small in size so that, from administrative point of view, the investigators may not be put to unnecessary troubles.

The sampling method also determines the size of the sample. When random sampling method is used, the samples have to be large. On the other hand if samples are selected through stratified sampling method, the reliability can be achieved even with the help of the small-sized samples.

Taking into consideration all these factors which influence the size of the sample, it was decided that an ideal sample would consist of six hundred students. This sample is small enough to avoid unnecessary expenditure and large enough to avoid intolerable sampling errors.

After deciding about the sampling method and the size of the sample, the universe selected was divided into different strata. The variables chosen for the study were considered to divide the universe. The variables chosen were (1) boys versus girls, (2) government versus private junior colleges, (3) residential versus non-residential junior colleges.

Taking the variable which compares residential and non-residential junior college students at first instance, the Universe was split into residential and non-residential junior colleges. An equal number of samples was taken from residential and non-residential colleges, i.e., 300 from residential junior colleges and 300 from non-residential junior colleges.

Taking the variable which compares government and private junior colleges, the Universe selected consisted of the senior intermediate students studying in government and private junior colleges of Andhra Pradesh. An equal number of samples was taken from both government and private junior colleges, i.e., 300 students from government colleges and 300 from private colleges.

To select the sub sample, the Random Sampling Method was considered. In this method all the units from all types of junior colleges, *viz.*, private and government junior colleges, and private and government residential junior colleges, were given equal importance. The individuals were chosen in such a way as each has an equal chance of being selected, and that each choice is independent of any other choice. Random sampling may be done with the help of many methods. The lottery method suggested by Best was used in this study. It was decided to select 24 colleges for the collection of sample. Out of these 24 colleges, 6 were private non-residential and 6 were government non-residential colleges, and 8 were private residential junior colleges and 4 were government residential junior colleges. As there is only one co-educational government residential junior college, girls are to be selected from that college only. The remaining residential junior college girls are to be selected from private residential junior colleges. In this method the names of private residential junior colleges were written on slips of equal size, the slips were wound round, well mixed, and kept in a container.

As per the schedule, 8 slips from the container were picked up to select eight private residential junior colleges. In the same manner other types of colleges were selected. From each college, it was decided to select 25 senior Intermediate students.

Following the above sampling procedure, 600 senior Intermediate students were selected as sample for this study. Out of these 600 senior intermediate students, 300 were from residential junior colleges and 300 were from non residential junior colleges. 300 boys were selected equal from residential and non-residential junior colleges. Girls were also selected from residential and non-residential colleges, but as there is only one government residential junior college which admits girls as co-educators equal number of girls were not selected equally from the government and private residential colleges. Twenty five girls were selected from the government residential junior college and 125 were selected from private residential junior colleges. The following table gives the details of the sample distribution.

Table 1 : Distribution of Sample

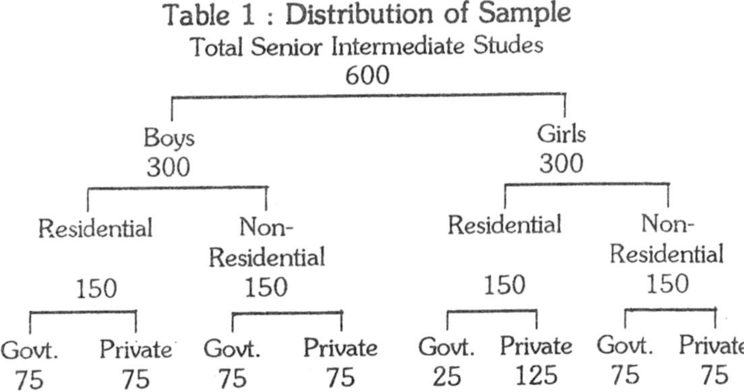

The sampling design employed thus involved not only the stratification of the universe but also random sampling technique to select samples from within the stratum.

Data Collection

Research tools are the sole factors in determining sound data and in drawing accurate conclusions about the problem in hand. The conclusions ultimately help in providing suitable remedial measures to the problem concerned.

The selection and use of tools can be done in two ways. The first one is to construct a tool independently by the researchers for their own study. Here, there are many problems in doing so. Preparation and standardization of a perfect tool itself is a major task, and one can say that it is a doctoral study itself. On construction of their own tools, Anand and Padma feel that 'a note of caution has to be struck when a researcher develops a tool for his study by merely pooling some items and does not subject it to the sophisticated techniques of tool construction. The result will be then obvious, a poor quality research'.

The second way of selection and use of tools is the right selection of tools from already standardized ones available in the field of study. Here also, it involves a tedious job in locating the tools and identifying their usefulness to the study on hand. Even then, this technique is very useful when a research work involves a good number of variables. some people believe that some of the instruments available do not measure upto their standards. Hence, new ones. In some instances, consideration should be given to the logistics of the situation. Lacking in the time and financial resources of a test and measurement organization or researcher, many researchers cannot expect to produce a better instrument. In these cases, the most logical procedure that can be followed is to choose the best instrument available for the purpose (Pearl, 1974).

To measure the achievement, marks of the Intermediate public examinations of the sample were taken. These marks were taken because these were achieved by the sample from the common public examination conducted by the board of Intermediate education, it being a testing organization established by the Government of Andhra Pradesh.

Data Analysis and Findings

The organization, analysis and interpretation of data and formulation of conclusions and generalizations are necessary steps to get a meaningful picture out of the raw information collected. The analysis and interpretation of data involve the objective material in the possession of the researcher and his subjective reactions and desires to derive from the data the inherent meanings in their relation to the problem.

The mass data collected through the use of various tools, need to be systematized and organized, i.e., edited, classified and tabulated before it can serve the purpose. Here editing implies the checking of gathered data for accuracy, utility and completeness; classifying refers to the dividing of the information into recording of the classified material in accurate mathematical terms. Analysis of data means studying the tabulated material in order to determine inherent facts or meanings. It involves breaking down the existing complex factors into simpler parts and putting the parts together in new arrangements for purposes of interpretation.

After the data collection was finished, it was analyzed keeping in view the objectives and hypotheses of the study. Physics and Chemistry marks of senior Intermediate public examination of each student were collected from the respective colleges. These raw data were put to statistical treatment. The hypotheses framed were statistically tested and accordingly accepted or rejected.

The total marks of senior Intermediate public examination of each student were taken to find out the achievement status of total sample as well as each sub-sample. The maximum score that a student can get is 120 and the minimum is 1. In the present study the highest score secured by a student was 118 and the lowest mark secured by a student was 42.

For the purpose of classification of achievement into 3 categories, *viz.*, low , average and high the following procedure was followed. As the sample was selected only from science group, the students scored very well. Hence the categorization was made as- a student who scored 42 and below (third class) was put in low achievement group, who scored between 43 and 81 (second and first classes) was kept in average achievement group, and who scored 82 and above (distinction) was placed in high achievement group.

The mean scores were used to identify the achievement status of total sample and to compare the sub-sample variation. The values of standard deviation were used to measure the spread or dispersion of scores in the distribution (Best). The critical ratios were calculated to test the significant difference in the means of the two sub-sample of each variable.

The chi-square (X^2) test of independence was applied for comparing the experimentally obtained results with those to be expected theoretically on some hypothesis (Garret, 1979).

Hypothesis 1

The Intermediate students will possess high achievement in science.

To test the validity of the Hypothesis 1, the total marks of all the samples were calculated to arrive at mean and standard deviation of the sample. The results are as follows :

Table 2: Achievement of the Whole Sample

Sample	*Sample Size*	*Mean*	*Standard Deviation*
Whole	600	10.34	24.08

It is clear, from the above table, that the Intermediate Science students studying in junior colleges were possessing high achievement. But, as per standard deviation, the dispersion of scores was high in the units of the sample.

The chi-square test of independence was applied to test the divergence of observed results from those expected theoretically.

Table 3 : Distribution of Achievement in the Whole Sample

Sample	*Size*	*Low*	*Average*	*High*	X^2
600	f_o	8	289	303	35.2*
	f_e	96	408	96	

* Significant at 0.01 level

f_o= frequency of occurrence of observed or experimentally determined facts

f_e= frequency of occurrence expected theoretically

As the chi-square test value was significant, the achievement of Intermediate students was not distributed normally. The achievement trend was tending towards high achievements.

The hypothesis that ***the Intermediate students will possess high achievement in science*** can be accepted.

Hypothesis 2

There will be a significant difference in the level of achievement of the students of residential and non-residential colleges.

To compare the difference in the level of achievement in residential and non-residential college students, the following statistical treatment was given.

Table 4 : Comparison of Achievement of Residential and Non-residential College Students

Variable	*Sample Size*	*Mean*	*Standard Deviation*	*Mean Difference*	*Critical Ratio*
Residential	300	107.63	20.54	27.6	8.32*
Non-Residential	300	80.03	23.79		

* Significant at 0.01 level

It is clear, from the above table, that there was a high significant difference in the level of achievement in the students studying in residential and non-residential colleges. The students of residential colleges were better in achievement than those of non-residential colleges.

As a high difference was seen in the level of achievement in the variables, the distribution of it was studied in both the sub-samples.

Table 5: Distribution of Achievement in Residential and Non-residential College Students.

Variable	*Sample Size*		*Low*	*Average*	*High*	X^2
Residential	300	f_o	1	89	210	67.59*
		f_e	48	204	48	
Non-Residential	300	f_o	3	142	155	19.86*
		f_e	48	204	48	

* Significant at 0.01 level

The distribution of achievement was not normal in both the cases. The achievement concentration in residential colleges was very high in high achievement group and it was almost equal in average and high achievement groups in non-residential colleges.

The hypothesis that ***there will be a significant difference in the level of achievement of the students of residential and non-residential junior colleges*** can be accepted.

Hypothesis 3

There will be a significant difference in the level of achievement of the students of private and government junior colleges.

A comparison was made to identify the difference in the level of achievement of the students studying in private and government colleges. The results are as shown in table 6.

As per the mean scores and value of critical ratio, there was a high difference in the level of achievement in the students of private and government colleges.

Table 6: Comparison of Achievement of Private and Government College Students

Variable	*Sample Size*	*Mean*	*Standard Deviation*	*Mean Difference*	*Critical Ratio*
Private	350	108.56	21.15	29.22	5.63*
Government	250	79.34	19.67		

* Significant at 0.01 level

As there was difference in the level of achievement in the sub-samples, it was tried to identify the distribution of achievement in the students of private and government colleges.

Table 7: Distribution of Achievement in Private and Government College Students

Variable	*Sample Size*		*Low*	*Average*	*High*	X^2
Private	350	f_o	1	131	218	129.44*
		f_e	56	238	56	
Government	250	f_o	2	149	99	13.72*
		f_e	40	170	40	

* Significant at 0.01 level

The distribution of achievement in the sub-sample was not normally distributed as the chi-square values were very highly significant. In private colleges the achievement concentration was in the high achievement group, but in the government colleges it was in the average achievement group.

The hypothesis that ***there will be a significant difference in the level of achievement of the students of private and government junior colleges*** can be accepted.

Hypothesis 4

There will be a significant difference in the level of achievement of boys and girls of junior colleges.

A comparison was made to identify the difference in the achievement of boys and girls, The data are as follows.

Table 8: Comparison of Achievement of Boys and Girls

Variable	*Sample Size*	*Mean*	*Standard Deviation*	*Mean Difference*	*Critical Ratio*
Boys	300	106.24	12.58	26.86	5.29*
Girls	300	79.38	11.42		

* Significant at 0.01 level

According to the mean scores and critical ratio there was a difference in the achievement of boys and girls.

As there was difference in the achievement of boys an girls, it was tried to identify the distribution of achievement in both the sub-samples.

Table 9: Distribution of Achievement in Boys and Girls

Variable	*Sample Size*		*Low*	*Average*	*High*	X^2
Boys	300	f_o	10	120	180	44.52*
		f_e	48	204	48	
Girls	300	f_o	2	161	137	39.36*
		f_e	48	204	48	

* Significant at 0.01 level

As per the chi-square value, boys were slightly better in achievement. In boys the achievement concentration was in high achievement group, where as it was in average achievement groups in girls.

The hypothesis that ***there will be a significant difference in the level of achievement of boys and girls of junior colleges*** can be accepted.

Conclusions and Discussion

Science is playing a major role in the present age to satisfy the needs and desires of the people and it has also became one of the major human activities. The search for truth became the dominant motive in the prosecution of science. It has been pursued for so many centuries and attracted ever wider extent of attention of very persisted group of people. Science is valued mostly for its practical advantages though it is also valued for gratified disinterested curiosity and as an object of great aesthetic charm. It is very obvious that the bulk of mankind value science clarity for the practical advantages it brings with it.

Science was given, a few decades back, a step-motherly treatment and was considered to be a subject meant for less promising students, the more promising students were encouraged to study the classics and mathematics as being more worthy and suitable subjects. Science has now established its claim to be placed in the school curriculum. It has now been recognized as a compulsory subject right from the elementary stage and now one of the core subjects at secondary and senior secondary stage. It has taken a good many years of active and persistent effort to reach this position.

Science, in curriculum, provides certain values which are not provided by any other subject. All the school subjects are taught because they provide liberal education, they are part of the equipment an preparation for life which we expect the school to give to its pupils so that they may play their part in the community as intellectual citizens. Science takes its place side by side with other school subjects as an essential element of one's education. It affords a knowledge of certain facts and laws and an insight into methods and data peculiar to the domain of science. However, the inclusion of any subject in the curriculum should satisfy the intellectual, utilitarian, vocational, cultural, moral and aesthetic values. Besides these, the teaching of science imparts training in the scientific method and develops scientific attitude and scientific aptitude, which are very valuable and at the same time are transferable to other situations of life. The scientific attitude plays a major role in science education, and in the lives of pupils pursuing science education. Identifying the importance of science education, the Science Policy Resolution (1958) of the Government of India stated 'the dominating feature of the contemporary world is the intense cultivation of science on a large scale and its application to meet the country's requirements. And science has now become a compulsory subject in school curriculum, and is trying to inculcate scientific attitude besides preparing the pupils for leading quality life.

Considering the importance of science in our life, this study has been taken up to identify the achievement of Intermediate students in science.

The present study has resulted in drawing the following conclusions which may be utilized in improving the present state of affairs in academic achievement.

The achievement of Intermediate science students studying in junior colleges was high. The distribution of achievement in Intermediate students was also tended towards high achievement.

Not many studies are available on the achievement of students as an independent study, particularly with the Intermediate students. Bhaskara Rao (1989) found that achievement in biology was average in the secondary school pupils. Rani (1980) found that the academic achievement of under-graduate engineering SC students was significantly lower than that of non-SC students. The study of Aruna (1981) also reported similar results. The result of the present study is contrary to the overall achievement of the Intermediate students.

The factors contributing to this high achievement are many and multifarious. The samples selected were in the socio-economically advanced districts of the state. And the colleges were well equipped with laboratory and library facilities. The staff was experienced and tne students were of science and mathematics who were known for their hard work, aspiring high goals. And most important thing is, there is a stiff competition among the residential and non-residential colleges, and private and government colleges for the admission of students, and of course, for their survival also. If the achievement is not good in residential and private colleges they wouldn't be self-sufficient in their maintenance. So, the administrators and the teachers work efficiently in cooperation to improve the academic achievement of their clientele. Contrary to this, for their survival, the members of the teaching staff of the government colleges are forced to improve the achievement of their students also by effective teaching.

The stiff competition among different categories of colleges, availability of adequate laboratory and library facilities, conducive learning atmosphere, experience and efforts of the teaching community, high educational aspirations of the students, socio-economic status of the locality have contributed for this high achievement in the Intermediate students. If these conditions are provided in all types of colleges, then there will be no question of chronic under-achievement and all the students will come out through the examinations with flying colours.

The achievement in the residential and non-residential junior colleges was different. The students studying in residential colleges were with high achievement, whereas those studying in non-residential colleges were with average achievement. The distribution of achievement in the sub-samples was also not normal. The concentration of achievement in residential colleges was very high in high achievement group, but it was concentrated in average and high achievement groups in non-residential colleges.

Bhaskara Rao (1989) also found that the pupils of residential schools were superior in achievement to their counter parts. The facilities that are available both in private residential junior colleges and Government residential junior colleges are no where available either in private aided or unaided non-residential colleges or in government non-residential colleges. The facilities such as good libraries, well furnished laboratories, teaching learning strategies, the study habits, time table of the institution, institutional set-up, administrator's capacity, advantages of residential system, rapport between teacher and taught media, expertise and commitment of the teaching community, intelligence and hard work of the student clientele might have helped in achieving a high achievement by the residential college students.

Srinivasa Rao and Subramanyam (1982) identified that among the school factors, accommodation, educational level and experience of teachers, availability of instructional material, books and reading room facilities have influence on reading attainment which is one of the prime factors of achievement. So, as far as possible, the above facilities should be extended to all non-residential colleges.

The achievement of the private and government college students was also with much difference. The achievement of private college students was high, whereas it was average in government colleges. As regards distribution of achievement, the achievement concentration in private colleges was very high in high achievement group, but it was high in average achievement group in government colleges.

Many people say that the conditions such as laboratory and library, class room climate, organizational set-up in private educational institution will be good. Desai (1979) and Hirunval observed a positive relationship between classroom climate and pupils academic achievement. Verma (1977) observed that the classes of the privately managed schools had a more learning-conducive climate. Rani (1980) and Shasidhar (1981) also concluded that the academic achievement was influenced by institutional factors. Another important thing is, the quality of teaching in private colleges will also be good as there are better teaching learning facilities.

The most quotable thing for this high achievement is that inferior teaching in private colleges will be questioned immediately without any delay, which is not possible in case of government colleges. The teachers will teach throughout a student's career in private colleges as the teacher works in the same institution for a long period without any transfers, and also he understands the flaws and potentialities of his students. All these factors will play a significant role in promoting achievement, and these may be adopted in government college also.

There was also a slight difference in the level of achievement in boys and girls studying in junior colleges, but this was less when compared with the variables-type and management of the colleges. The boys were with high achievement where as the girls were with high-average achievement. The achievement distribution in the sub-samples was also different. The achievement concentration of boys was high in high achievement group,

where as it was slightly high in average achievement group in girls. This result states that there was not much influence of sex on achievement.

The findings of Thakur (1972) and Second International Science Study (1988) indicate that the boys were superior to girls in science achievement. Contrary to this the same Second International Science Study stated that girls scored higher than boys in biology in some countries an it also concluded that the differences between boys and girls in achievement were greater in the physical sciences than in the life sciences. The result of this study and the contradictory findings of the above mentioned studies indicate that if proper facilities are provided, both boys and girls will achieve equally well.

Suggestions for Further Research

This study brings to light some new areas to be studied by the further researchers. The areas and variables which are not covered by this study may be put to test to enlighten the other factors associated with the achievement and the association between achievement and other psycho-sociological variables. Hence, the researchers may think of the following areas to study in detail.

1. Studies on achievement may be extended to other educational levels, *viz.*, primary, secondary, degree, post graduation, at district as well as state level.
2. Studies on achievement in independent subjects may also be taken up.
3. Studies may be taken up to find out the effect of independent variables on dependent variables in the cases of controlled and experimental groups as this study has not used any controlled groups and variables.
4. Studies may be conducted on achievement to identify its association with other psychological variables in order to enhance the achievement.
5. Studies may be carried out to find out the effect of environmental factors on achievement and its associated variables.
6. Studies may be conducted to find out the influence of locale of the institution, medium of instruction on achievement.
7. Studies may be taken up on the role of psychological variables of teachers in enhancing the achievement.

Bibliography

Agin, M.L. (1974). "Education for Scientific Literacy : A Conceptual Frame of Reference and Some Applications". *Science Education*. 58: 403-415.

Alpern, Moris L. (1964, October). "The Ability to Test Hypotheses". *Science Education*. 30: 220-229.

Approach Paper on Science and Mathematics in General Education. Report of the working group on Science & Mathematics, September 1985. Department of Education in Science & Mathematics, National Council of Education Research and Training, New Delhi.

Atkinson, J. Myron and R. Will Burnell, "Science Education". *Enclyclopedia of Educational Research*, 4th ed. 1192-1205.

Bernal, J.D, (1970). *Science and Industry in the Nineteenth Century*. Bloomington : Indiana University press.

Best, John W. (1982). Research in Education, 4th ed. New Delhi : Prentice Hall of India Pvt. Ltd.

Bettencourt, Antonio (1992), "On what it means to understand science". Second International Conference on *History and Philosophy of Science in Science Education*. Queen's University, Canada.

Bhandula, N., P. C. Chadha, S. Sharma and M.P. Bhasin (1985). *Teaching of Science*. Ludhiana: Prakash Brothers.

Bhaskara Rao, D. (1982). *An Evaluative Study of the New Science Curriculum at Upper Primary Level in Andhra*

Pradesh. Master of Education Dissertation, Nagarjuna University.

Bhaskara Rao, D. (1982, June). "Education for Individual Responsibility". *Educational India*. 48: 185-187.

Bhaskara Rao, D. (1982, October). "An Evaluative Study of the new Science Curriculum at Upper Primary Level in Andhra Pradesh". *Experiments in Education*. X: 147-149.

Bhaskara Rao, D. (1983, July). "Teacher: The Supreme of Mankind". *Education*. 63 : 193-196.

Bhaskara Rao, D. (1984, February). "Private Educational Institutions". *The Educational Review*. XC : 34-36.

Bhaskara Rao, D. (1985, August). "Effective Communication in Teaching". *Experiments in Education*. XIII : 109-111.

Bhaskara Rao, D. (1986, February). "Utilisation of Community Resources in Science Teaching". *Junior Scientist*. 23: 5-6.

Bhaskara Rao, D. (1987, October 10-12). "Science Education in Secondary Schools: A Reflection". *National Conference on New Education Policy—Its Need & Concept*. Department of Education, Hindu College, Moradabad, India.

Bhaskara Rao, D. (1988, September). "An Evaluative Study of the Teaching efficiency of Prospective Biological Science Teachers". *School Science*. XXVI : 17-20.

Bhaskara Rao, D. (1989). *A Comparative Study of Scientific Attitude, Scientific aptitude and Achievement in Biology at Secondary School Level*. Ph.d. Thesis, Osmania University.

Bhaskara Rao, D. (1989). *Dhrusya Sravana Bhodhapankaranamulu* (Audio Visual Teaching Aids). Guntur : Nagarjuna Publishers.

Bhaskara Rao, D. (1989, October). "Objectives of Science". *Science Promoter*. 2: 701-703.

Bhaskara Rao, D. (1990, June). "Science Education in Secondary Schools". *Experiments in Education*. XVIII : 163-166.

Bhaskara Rao, D. (1991, September 16-18). "Biological Basis

of Learning". Second International Conference on *Differentiated Psychology of Learning—Its Fundamentals and Application*, Martin Luther University, Halle, Germany.

Bhaskara Rao, D. (1992, August 2-8). "Teaching Learning Strategies in Environmental Education". *Eighth Asian symposium of the International Council of Associations for science Education on Science Education for a Changing World.* International Council of Association for Science Education, Colombia, Sri Lanka.

Bhaskara Rao, D. (1992, July 8-14). "Quality or Equality". *Eighth Congress of World Council of Comparative Education Societies on Education, Democracy and Development.* Charles University, Prague, Czechoslovakia.

Bhaskara Rao, D. (1992, May 11-15). "Scientific Attitude in Secondary School Pupils". *Second International Conference on History and Philosophy of Science and Science Teaching*, Queen's University, Kingston, Ontario, Canada.

Bhaskara Rao, D. (1992, October 11-14). "Underachievement : Identification, Diagnosis and Treatment". *Third European Conference of the European Council for High Ability on Competence and Responsibility.* University of Munich, Munich, Germany.

Bhaskara Rao, D. (1992, October). "Biological Basis of Learning". *Journal of Educational Research and Extension.* 29 : 65-75.

Bhaskara Rao, D (1993). *Vignanasasthra Bodhana* (Teaching of Science). Guntur: Nagarjuna Publishers.

Bhaskara Rao, D. (1993, August 20-25). "Development of Educational Television in India". International Conference Teleteaching 93 on *Learning and Working Independent of Time and Distance.* Foundation for Continuing Education of the Norwegian Institute of Technology, Trondheim, Norway.

Bhaskara Rao, D. (1993, January 3-8). "Teachers's Role in Dealing with Learning difficulties". *International Conference on Science Education in Developing Countries: From Theory to Practice.* The Amos De-Shalit Israeli Science Teaching Centre, Jerusalem, Israel.

Bhaskara Rao, D. (1993, November 11-14). "Education for Peace-Need of the Day". Second Conference of the European Peace Research Association on *Improving European Security: Threats and Responsibilities*. Budapest, Hungary.

Bhaskara Rao, D. (1993, October 1-4). "Disarmament". Fifth International Castiglioncello Conference on *Conflicts and Disarmament*. Union of Scientists for Disarmament, Italy.

Bhaskara Rao, D. (1993, September 5-9). "Education vis-a-vis Democracy". Fourth School Year 2020 Conference *The European Educational House*. IMTEC & COMED. Bogensee, Germany.

Bhaskara Rao, D. (1994). *Jeevasathra Bodhana* (Teaching of Biology). Guntur: Creative Press.

Bhaskara Rao, D. (1994). *Scientific Aptitude*. New Delhi : Ashish Publishing House.

Bhaskara Rao., D. (1994). *Scientific Attitude*. Ambala Cantt: The Associated Publishers.

Bhaskara Rao, D. (1994, April 6-9). "Creativity and Academic Achievement". European Council for Highe Ability's International Workshop on *Creative Potential—Exploring and Developing*, University degli studi di Pavia, Pavia, Italy.

Bhaskara Rao, D. (1994, October 8-11). "Special Activities for Talented in General Classes". Fourth Conference of the European Council for High Ability on *Nurturing Talent: Individual Needs and Social Ability*. University of Nijmegen, Nijmegen, The Netherlands.

Bhaskara Rao, D. (1995). *Vidhya Manovignana Sasthram* (Educational Psychology). Guntur: Creative Press.

Bhaskara Rao, D. and D. Pushpa Latha (1994). *Achievement in Biology*. New Delhi: Discovery Publishing House.

Bhaskara Rao, D. and D. Vijaya Lakshmi (1982, August). "An Evaluative Study of the New Science Syllabus of class VII in A.P." *Educational India*. 49: 19-22.

Bhaskara Rao, D., D. Eliah and G. S. Rao (1987, April). "Pedagogic Aptitude of In-service and Pre-service Teachers". *The Educational Review*. XCIII : 61-64.

Bhaskara Rao, D., G. S. Rao and D. V. D. Malleswari (1987, January). "Teachers Opinions towards the Appeal of Pictorial Representations and Motivational Quality of Suggested Activities in Science Text Books at Primary Level in Andhra Pradesh". *Educational India.* 53 : 102-104.

Bhaskara Rao, D., G. S. Rao and L. Rathaiah (1988, September 27). "The Science teacher has a definite role". *The Hindu.*

Bhaskara Rao, D., G. S. Rao and V. B. Reddy (1986, December). "Conceptulisation Facility in General Science Text Book of Class VII in Andhra Pradesh . "*Educational India.* 53: 87-90.

Bhaskara Rao, D., L. Rathaiah, G. S. Rao and M. V. Lakshmi (1987, August). "Attitudes of Urban Graduate Science Teachers Towards the use of Visual Aids in Class Room Teaching." *The Educational Review.* XCII : 13-135.

Bhatia, K.K. (1991). *Measurement and Evaluation in Education.* Ludhiana: Prakash Brothers.

Bishop, Alan (1985). "The Social Construction of Meaning : A Significant Development for Mathematical Education?". *For the Learning of Mathematics.* 5, 24-28.

Biswas, A. and J.C. Aggrawal (1987). *Encyclopedic Dictionary and Directory of Education*, Vol. 1. New Delhi : The Academic Publishers (India).

Biswas, A. and S. Agrawal (1987). *Indian Educational Documents since Independence.* New Delhi : The Academic Publishers (India).

Biswas, A. and S.P. Agrawal (1986). *Development of Education in India.* New Delhi: Concept Publishing Co.

Bloom, Benjamin S., ed. (1959). *Taxonomy of Educational Objectives, Hand Book I: Cognitive Domain.* New York: Longman, Green and Co.

Brandwein, Paul F., Fletcher G. Watson and Paul B. Blackwood (1958). *A Book of Research Methods.* New York : Harcourt, Brace World, Inc.

Brovery, D.J. (1980). "Science Among Ordinary Citizens". *Journal of College Science Teaching.* 10:88-91.

Brown , H.I. (1977). *Perception, Theory and Commitment: The New Philosophy of Science.* Chicago : The University of Chicago Press.

Bruner, J.S. (1983). *The Process of Education.* Cambridge : Harvard University Press.

Brunkhorst, Herbert K. and Robert E. Yager (1986, December). "A New Rationale for Science Education". *The Education Digest.* 24-27.

Bryan, I.F. and E.A. Locke (1967). 'Goat Setting as a Measure of Increasing Motivation', *Journal of Applied Psychology* 51: 274-277.

Buch, M.B., Chief Editor (1987). *Third Survey of Research in Education.* 1979-1983. New Delhi: National Council of Educational Research.

Buck, M.B., Chief Editor (1987). *Third Survey of Research in Education.* New Delhi; National Council of Educational Research and Training.

Buch M.B., editor (1979). *Second Survey of Research in Education.* Baroda: Society for Educational Research and Development.

Burmester, Mary Alice (1953, March), "The Construction and Validation of a Test to Measure some of the Inductive Aspects of Scientific Thinking". *Science Education.* 37: 131-140.

Burnett, R. will (1960). *Teaching Science in the Secondary Schools.* New York: Holt, Rinehart and Winston.

Bybee, R. (1979). "Science Education and the Emerging Ecological Society". *Science Education.* 63: 95-109.

Bybee, R., N. Harms, B. Ward and R. Yager (1980). "Science, Society and Science Education". *Science Education.* 64: 377-395.

Caldwell, Otis W. and Francis D. Curtis (1943). *Everyday Science.* Boston: Ginn and Co.

Canant, J.B. (1947). *On Understanding Science:* An Historical Approach. New Heaven, Connectiant: Yale University Press.

Carleton, R. (1961). "Editorial". *The Science Teacher.* 28:4.

Chikara, M.S. and S. Sharma (1985). *Teaching of Biology.*

Ludhiana: Prakash Brothers.

Collingwood, R.G. (1982). *An Autobiography.* Oxford: Clarendon Press.

Das, N.C. (1985). "A Comparative Study of the Achievement in Science of High School Students of Urban and Rural Areas". *Indian journal of Community Guidance.* 2: 83-86.

Das, R.C. (1985). *Science Teaching in Schools.* New Delhi: Sterling Publishers.

Desai, D.B. and Ameeta Govind (1979). *Studies in Achievement Motivation.* Baroda: Centre for Advanced Study in Education, M.S. University of Baroda.

Dewey, J. (1934). "The supreme Intellectual Obligation". Science Education. 18:1-4.

Digumarti (1994, January). "The Mind". Science Promoter. 7: 4-9

Downing, Elliot R. (1936, October). "Some Results of a Test on Scientific Thinking". *Science Education.* 20:121.

Driver, R.,E. Guesne and A. Tiberghien, eds. (1985). *Children's Ideas in Science.* Milton Keynes: Open University Press.

Durant and Durant. *The Story of Civilisation.* New York: Simon and Schuster.

English, H.B. and A.C. English (1958). *A Comprehensive Dictionary of Psychoanalytical Terms.* London; Longmans.

Fergusan, George A. (1981). *Statistical Analysis in Psychology and Education.* 5th ed. Tokyo : McGraw-Hill International Book Co.

Festinger, I. (1942). "Theoretical Interpretation of Shifts in Level of Aspiration', *Psychological Review* 49: 235-250.

Festinger, Leon and Katz Daniel. (1976). *Research Methods in the Behavioural Sciences.* Amerind Publishing co.

Frankfort, H., H.A. Frankfort, J. Wilson and T. Jacobson (1946). *Before Philosophy : The Intellectual Adventure of Ancient Man.* Baltimore: Penguin Books.

Freeman, Frank S. (1965). *Theory and Practice of Psychological Testing,* 3rd ed. Calcutta: Oxford & IBH Publishing Co.

Gadamer, Hans-Georg (1981). *Reason in the Age of Science.* Cambridge: MIT Press.

Gage, N.L. (1966). *Handbook of Research on Teaching*. Chicago: Rand McNally & Co.

Garret, Henry E. (1979). *Statistics in Psychology and Education*. Bombay; Peffer and Simons Pvt. Ltd.

General Science Sub-committee of the Science Masters' Association (1960). *Report on the Teaching of General Science*. London; John Murray.

Goldstein, T. (1980). *Dawn of Modern Science*. Boston; Houghton Miffin Co.

Good, C.V., ed. (1959). *Dictionary of Education*. New York; McGraw-Hill Book Co.

Goode, William J. and Paul K. Hatt (1983). *Methods in Social Research*. Tokyo: McGraw-Hill International Book Co.

Gravetter, Frederick J. and Larry B. Wallnau (1987). *Statistics for the Behavioral Sciences*. New Delhi : MrGraw-Hill Publishing Co. Ltd.

Green, T. L. (1965). *The Teaching of Biology in Tropical Secondary Schools*, vol. X of the UNESCO Handbook on the Teaching of Science in Tropical Countries. London: Oxford University Press.

Guilford, J.P. (1987). *Psychometric Methods*. New Delhi : Tata McGraw-Hill Publishing Co. Ltd.

Gupta, Arun Kumar (1985, October). "*Differential Scientific aptitude abilities and Scholastic Achievement*". Indian Educational Review XX : 151-157.

Hanson, Norwood R. (1958) *Patterns of Discovery : An Inquiry into the Conceptual Foundations of Science*. New York : Cambridge University Press.

Hazen, R and J. Trefil (1991). *Science Matters:* Achieving Scientific Literacy. New York : Doubleday.

Heiss, Eldwood D., Ellsworth S. Obourn and Charles W. Hoffman (1950). *Modern Science Teaching*. New York: The MacMillan Co.

Henry, Nelson B., ed. (1960). *Rethinking Science Education*. The fifty ninth Yearbook of the National Society for the Study of Education, Part-1. Distributed by the University of Chicago Press, Chicago, Illinois.

Hurd, P.D. (1970). "Scientific Enlightenment for an Age of

Science". *The Science Teacher.* 37 : 13-15.

Hutchings, Donal, ed. (1966, June). *Towards More Creative Science.* New College Conference. Oxford: Pegamon Press.

Jain, N.K. (1982). *History of Science and Scientific Method.* New Delhi : Oxford & IBH Publishing Co.

Janvier, C., ed. (1987). *Problems of Representation in the Teaching and Learning of Mathematics.* Hillsdane, NJ : L. Erlbaum Associates.

Jayaswal, Sita Ram (1968). *Techniques and Tests in Psychology and Education.* Lucknow: Prakashan Kendra.

Jenkins, E. W. (1985). "Science Education, History Of". *The International Encyclopedia of Educational Research and Studies.* 8: 4453-4456.

Jocabson, Willard J. and Rodney L. Doran. (1988). *Science Achievement in the United States and Sixteen Countries.* The International Association for the Evaluation of Educational Research, Second IEA Science Study. Teachers College, Columbia University, New York.

Jones, R.F., ed. (1937). *Francis Bacon Essays, Advancement of Learning, New Atlantis, and Other Pieces.* New York: The Odyssey press. Inc.

Jose, K.M. (1987). *A Comparative Study of the Biology Achievement of High, Average, and Low Science Aptitude of Secondary School Pupils.* M.Ed. Thesis, University of Calicut.

Karla, R.M. (1976). *Innovations in Science Teaching.* New Delhi : Oxford & IBH Publishing Co.

Kaur, Gursharan (1989). *Underachievement : Identification Diagnosis and Treatment.* New Delhi : Commonwealth Publishers.

Kennedy, P.J. and A. Loria, (1980, September 1-6). *Proceedings of the International Conference on Education for Physics Teaching.* TRIESTE. The International Commission on Physics Education, Physics Department, University of Edinburgh, Scotland.

Kerlinger, Fred N. (1964). *Foundations of Behavioural Research.* Holt, Rinehart & Winston.

Klopfer, L. (1969). "The Teaching of Science and the History of Science". *Journal of Research in Science Teaching*. 6 : 87-95.

Kohli, V.K. *How to Teach Science.* Ambala City : Vivek Publishers

Kropotkine, P.A. (1925). *Mutual Aid : A Factor in Evolution.* New York: Knopf.

Kuhn, T.S. (1980). *The Structure of Scientific Revolutions,* 2nd Ed. Chicago : The University of Chicago Press.

Kundu, C.L. and D.N. Tutoo (1985). *Educational Psychology.* New Delhi : Sterling Publishers Pvt. Ltd.

Kuppuswamy, B. (1980). *An Introduction to Social Psychology.* New Delhi: Asia Publishing House (P) Ltd.

Lacey, A.L., (1966). *Guide to Science Teaching.* Belment, California: Wadsworth Publishing Co., Inc.

Liebert, Robert M. (1979). Rita Wicks Poluos and Gloria Strauss Marmor, *Development Psychology,* 2nd ed. New Delhi: Prentice Hall of India Pvt. Ltd.

Link, F. (1967). "An Approach to a more Adequate Systems of Evaluation in Science". T*he Science Teacher.* 34: 20-24.

Lowel, E.K. and J.W. Atkinson (1953). The Effect of Need for Achievement on Learning and Speed of performance'. *Journal of Psychology* 33: 31-40.

Malla Reddy, M. (1988). *Student Unrest- A Socio-psychological Study.* Department of Education, Osmania University, Hyderabad.

Matyas, M.L., K.G. Dobbin and B.J. Fraser, eds. (1989). *Looking into Windows; Qualitative Research in Science Education.* Washington D.C.: American Association for the Advancement of Science.

Maybury, Robert H. and Adolph Y. Wilbrun, "*Science Education, International*". The Encyclopedia of Education. 8: 107-117.

Miller, David F. and Clenn W. Blaydes. (1962). *Methods and Materials for Teaching the Biological Sciences.* Bombay: Tata McGraw Hill Publishing Co. Pvt Ltd.

Ministry of Human Resource Development, Department of

Education, Government of India (1985). *Challenges of Education—a Policy Perspective.*

Ministry of Human Resource Development, Department of Education, Government of India (1986). *National Policy on Education - 1986.*

Muthayya, B.C. (1962). 'Level of Aspiration and Intelligence of High Achievers and Low Achievers in Scholastic Field', *Journal of Psychological Research* 9 : 3.

Nair, A.S. and S. Joseph (1978). *An Experimental Study of the Overlap of Intelligence and Science Aptitude with Educational Outcomes in Biology Measured Using Host's Taxonomy.* Department of Education, University of Kerala.

National Scheme of Inservice Training of School Teachers (1987). *Resource Material, Part I, General.* New Delhi: National Council of Educational Research and Training.

National Scheme of In-service Training of School Teachers (1987). *Resource Material part II, Secondary.* New Delhi: National Council of Educational Research and Training.

National Science Teachers Association (1962). "Curriculum Development in Science". *The Science Teacher.* 29: 32-37.

Okey, James R. (1982). "The Scientific Attitude and Science Education : A Critical Reappraisal". *Science Education.* 66: 109-121.

Orlich, D. (1964). "The Dawn of Scientific Epistemology: 1564-1964". *Journal of Research in Science Teaching.* 2: 95-99.

Osbrone, R. and P. Freyberg. eds (1985). Learning in Science: *The Implications of Children's Science.* London; Heinemann.

Pal, G. (1982). *An Enquiry into the Factors involved in the Learning of Science by Adolescent Pupils.*

Patnaik, Nalini Prabha. (1986, March). "Achievement in General Science of Class V Children of Berhampur, Orissa- A Research Study". *School Science* XXIV : 47-50.

Pearl, Richard E. (1974). "The Present Status of Scientific Attitude Measurement; History, Theory and Availability of Measurement', *School Science and Mathematics* LXXIV: 375-381.

Pella, M., G. O' Hearn and C. Gale (1966). "Scientific Literacy - Its Referents". *The Science Teacher.* 33:44.

Peterson, Rita W. and Gaylon R. Carlson (1979). "A Summary of Research in Science Education 1977". *Science Education.* 63.

Pillai, Kamala S. (1986, December). "The Relative Efficiency of Science Aptitude and Intelligence to predict Biology Achievement". *Experiments in Education.* XIV : 171-175.

Prather, J. Preston (1992). "History of the Invention and Implementation of the Concept of Science Education". Second International Conference on *History and Philosophy of Science in Science Education.* Queen's University, Canada.

Programme of Mass Orientation for School Teachers (1988). *Inservice Teacher Education Package.* Col I: For Primary School Teachers. New Delhi : National Council of Educational Research and Training.

Programme of Mass Orientation for School Teachers (1988). *Inservice Teacher Education Vol II:* For Upper primary & Secondary School Teachers. New Delhi : National Council of Educational Research and Training.

Rai, B. C. (1983). *Methods of Teaching Science.* Lucknow; Prakashan Kendra.

Ramkumar, V. (1972). 'An Investigation into the relationship of size of family to Self-concept and Academic Achievement'. *Edu. and Psych. Review.* XII : 107-113.

Rathaiah, L and D. Bhaskara Rao (1990). 'Residential Collegeelu Vidyarthulni Aakarshinchadaniki Karanalemity'. *Udayam.*

Rathaiah, L. and D. Bhaskara Rao (1990). 'Residential Colleges : relevance in the present system'. *The Hindu* : 18.

Rathaiah, L. and D. Bhaskara Rao (1990). 'Role of residential colleges'. *Indian Express* : 7.

Rathaiah, L. and D. Bhaskara Rao. (1994). *Achievement Correlates.* Ambala Cantt. ; The Indian Publications.

Reader's Digest (1984). *Great Illustrated Dictionary, A-K.* London: The Readers Digest Association Ltd.

Reif, Frederick. (1986), November). "Scientific Approaches to Science Education". *Physics Today.* 38-44.

Richardson, John S., Stanely E. Williamson and Donald W. Stotler (1968). *The Education Science Teachers.* Columbus, Ohio: Charles E. Merril Publishing Company.

Rummel, J. Francis (1958). *An Introduction to Research Procedures in Education.* New York: Harper and Brothers.

Salmon, W.C. (1967). *The Foundations of Scientific Influence.* Pittsburgh; University of Pittsburgh.

Santillana, G. de (1961). *The Origins of Scientific Thought.* New York : Mentor Books, The New American Library.

Saunders, H. N. (1959). *The Teaching of General Science in Tropical Secondary Schools.* Vol. VII of the UNESCO Handbooks on the Teaching of Science in Tropical Countries. London: Oxford University Press.

Saxena, K.N.A. (1963). "A Comparative Study of the Achievement in Science of Urban and Rural Students". *Journal of Education and Psychology,* 21 : 38-44.

Schibeci, R. A. (1983, October). "Selecting Appropriate Attitudinal Objectives for School Science". *Science Education.* 67 : 595-603.

Science Education in Asia and the Pacific (1984). Bulletin of the UNESCO Regional Office for Education in Asia and the Pacific, Number 25. Bangkok : UNESCO Regional Office for Education in Asia and the Pacific.

Sears, P.S. (1940). 'Level of Aspiration in Academically Successful and Unsuccessful Children', *Journal of Abnormal and Social Psychology* 35 : 498-536.

Secondary Modern Schools Sub-committee of the Science Masters' Association. (1964). *Secondary Modern Science Teaching, Part I.* London : John Murray.

Sharma, B.A.V., D.R. Prasad and P. Satyanaryana (1989). editors. *Research Methods in Social Sciences.* New Delhi : Sterling Publishers Private Limited.

Sharma , H.L. (1989). *School Science Education in India.* New Delhi: Commonwealth Publishers.

Sharma, R. C. (1984). *Modern Science Teaching.* Delhi; Dhanpat Rai & Sons.

Sharma, Radha R. (1985). *Enhancing Academic Achievement*

- *Role of Some Personality Factors.* New Delhi : Concept Publishing Co.

Shukla, U. C. (1977). *Kothari Commission Report.* Lucknow; Parkashan Kendra.

Singh, Raja Roy (1986). *Education in Asia and the Pacific - Retrospect; Prospect.* Bangkok : UNESCO Regional office for Education in Asia and the Pacific.

Skaria, S. (1984). *A Study of the Attainment of Essential Concepts in Biology in Relation to Science Aptitude of Secondary School Pupils.* Master of Education thesis, University of Calicut.

Smith, Edward W., Stanely W. Krouse, Jr. and Mark M. Atkinson (1967). *The Educator's Encyclopedia.* Englewood Cliffs, N J : Prentice Hall, Inc.

Sood, J.K. (1987). *Teaching Life Sciences - A book of Methods.* Chandigarh : Kohli Publishers.

Sood, J.K. (1989). *New Directions in Science Teaching.* Chandigarh: Kohli Publishers.

Sood, J. K., ed. (1978). *Emerging Perspectives in Science Education Research.* Ajmer : Regional College of Education.

Sreekumar, S. (1972). *A Comparative Study of Science Interest, Science Aptitude and Science Achievement in Science Club Members and Non-members of High School.* Master of Education Dissertation, University of Kerala.

Stromsworld, S. A. and C.G. Wrenn (1948), 'Counselling Students towards School Adjustment'. *Educational and Psychological Measurement* 8: 57-63.

Sujatha, Kumari B. (1987). *The Relative Efficiency of Science Aptitude, Science Aptitude, Science Interest and Attitude towards Science in Predicting Biology Achievement of Secondary School Pupils.* Master of education thesis, University of Calicut.

Sukhia, S.P., P.V. Mehrotra and R.N. Mehrotra (1980). *Elements of Educational Research.* New Delhi : Allied Publishers Pvt. Ltd.

Sumangala, V. (1989, March). "Effect of Attitude towards Mathematics and Sex on Achievement in Mathematics.

Experiments in Education. XVI; 156-161.

Sundararajan, S. (1989, March). "Higher Secondary Students' Achievement in Biology". *Experiments in Education*. XVII: 58-66.

Swarnamma, G. (1978). *An Enquiry into the Teaching of Biology in the Upper Primary Schools in Kerala*. Ph.D. Thesis, Kerala University.

Taylor, R.G. (1964). 'Personality Traits and Discrepant Achievement', *Journal of Counseling Psychology*. 11: 76-82.

Thakur, R.S. (1972). *A Study of the Scholastic Achievement of Secondary School Pupils in Bihar*. D. Litt. Thesis, Bihar University.

Thampy, M.P. (1984). *A Study of the Interaction of Science Aptitude and Attitude towards Science on Biology Achievement of Secondary School Pupils*. Master of Education thesis, University of Calicut.

The Readers Digest (1962). *Great Encyclopedic Dictionary*. Vol. 1, A-L. London : The Reader's Digest Association.

Thurber, Walter A. and Alfred T. Collette (1963). *Teaching Science in Today's Secondary Schools*, 3rd ed. Boston: Allyn and Bacon, Inc.

Underhill, O.E. (1941). *The origins and Development of Elementary School Science*. New York : Scott Foresman and Company.

UNESCO (1974). *Learning to be*. New Delhi: National Council of Educational Research and Training.

Vaidya, Narendra (1976). *The Impact Science Teaching*. New Delhi: Oxford & IBH Publishing Co.

Vaidya, Narendra and J.S. Rajput, eds. (1977). *Reshaping our School Science Education*. New Delhi : Oxford & IBH Publishing Co.

Vaidya, Narendra. (1967). *Problem Solving in Science*. Delhi: S. Chand & Co.

Venkata Rao, P. and D. Bhaskara Rao. (1988). *A Text Book of Zoology - Junior Intermediate*, Revised Edition. Guntur: Vigyan Publishers.

Venkata Rao, P. and D. Bhaskara Rao. (1988). *A Text Book of Zoology- Senior Intermediate*, Revised Edition. Guntur:

Vigyan Publishers.

Vessel, M.F. (1965). *Elementary School Science Teaching.* New Delhi : Prentice Hall of India (Pvt) Ltd.

Victor, Edward and Marjorie S. Lemar (1967). *Readings in Science Education for the Elementary School.* New York: The Macmilan Co.

von Glasersfeld, Ernst (1983). "On the Concept of Interpretation". *Poetics.* 12 : 207-218

Walberg, Herbert J. and Geneva D. Haertel, Eds. (1990). *The International Encyclopedia of Educational Evaluation.* Oxford : Pergamon Press.

Wanchoo, V.N. and T.N. Raina, eds. (1976). *Research in Science & Mathematics Education.* Ajmer : Regional College of Education.

Wanchoo, V.N., ed. (1982). *World Views on Science Education.* Oxford & IBH Publishing Co.

Washton, Nathan S. (1961). *Scienece Teaching in the Secondary Schools.* New York : Harper & Brothers.

Wells, H.G., (1961). *The Outline of History.* New York : Garden City Books.

Whitehead, A.N. (1941). *Science and Modern World.* New York : The MacMillan Company.

Williams, S.S. (1979). "A Comparative Study of the Achievement of Rural and Urban Secondary Pupils in General Science". *Journal of the Institute of Educational Research.* 3: 33-34.

Williams, Sarah S. (1987). "A Comparative Study of Pupils' Achievement in some of the Instructional Objectives in teaching General Science". *Experiments in Education.* XV: 67-73.

Yadav. K. (1993). *Teaching of Life Sciences.* New Delhi: Anmol Publishers.

Yadav, M.S. (1992). *Teaching of Science.* New Delhi: Anmol Publishers.

Young, Pauline V. and Calvin F. Schmid (1968). *Scientific Social Surveys and Research.* New Delhi : Prentice Hall of India Pvt. Ltd.

Appendices

TEST PAPERS

INTERMEDIATE
(Second year— Year-wise Scheme)
Part III—Physical Sciences
PHYSICS—Paper II

Time : 3 Hrs. Max. Marks : 60

Read the followign instructions carefully :

1. All questions are compulsory.
2. Questions form Sl. Nos. 1to 18 are of "Very Short" answer type. Each question carries one mark. Every answer may be limited to a word, phrase or a sentence. *Answer these questions continuously one after the other in the same serial order. Otherwise they will not be valued.*
3. Questions from Sl. Nos. 19 to 28 are of "Short" answer type. Each question carries 3 marks. Every answer may be limited to 50 to 60 words.
4. Questions with serial Nos. 29 and 30 are of "Long" answer type. Each question carries 6 marks. Every answer may be limited to 250 words.

I

1. State Huygen's principle of wave theory.
2. What type of wave is the sound wave in air ?
3. What is the instrument in which the directive property of a magnet used ?

4. If θ_1 and θ_2 are the deflections prodcued by a magnet placed at the same distance from the centre in tan-A and tan-B positions, what is the relation between them?
5. Can you conduct resonating air columns experiment on the moon?
6. Who discovered X-rays/
7. What is the electric potential of the earth?
8. What are Fraunhofer lines?
9. The pole strength of two poles are doubled and the distance between the poles is halved. How is the force between them affected?
10. If you are given lenses of local length 100cm, 50cm, 5cm, 2cm, which lenses do you select to construct a telescope?
11. What is the colour of the positive column when the discharge tube contains neon?
12. What happens to the cosmic ray Intensity as altitude increases?
13. Which is the sure test of magnetism?
14. What is the S.I. unit of Resistance?
15. On what principle Atom bomb is based ?
16. What are the atoms fo the same atomic number but different atomic masses called?
17. What is the physical quantity which has electron-volt as unit?
18. How do you account for the energy of the sun?

II

19. Mention any three properties of cathode rays.
20. Draw a neat labelled ray diagram of ramsden eye-piece.
21. What is the distinction between Proton and photon?
22. What is the difference between simple and compound Microscopes?
23. Write three peaceful uses of atomic energy.
24. Explain the types of magnetic substances in the nature.
25. Distinguish between the Crystalline and Amorphous solids.

26. What is the difference between a resistance-box and a rheostat?

27. Explain "Seebeck-effect".

28. The magnification of a telescope is 24. If the angle subtended by the object at objective is 30°, what is the angle subtended by the image at the eye ?

III

29. What is Resonance? Describe and experiment to determine the velocity of sound in air by the resonating air columns method.

If the velocity of sound in gas at 10°C is 330 ms^{-1}, find its velocity at 110°C.

OR

Starting from Newton's equation for velocity of sound in gases, deduce the expression for the velocity of sound in terms of absolute temperature.

If a person standign by the side of a well, wants to hear the echo, wht should be the minimum depth of the well? [Velocity of sound in air at atmospheric temperature 330ms^1]

30. State Kirchhoff's Laws. Using Kirchhoff's laws, deduce the conditions for balcnce of wheatsone's bridge.

In a Wheatstone's bridge resistances are P=2Ω, Q=4Ω, R=6Ω then what is the value of "S" when the deflection in the galvanometer is zero?

OR

Describe the construction and working of a moving coil glavanometer. Deduce the relation between the electric current and deflection of the coil.

INTERMEDIATE
(Second Year—Year-wise Scheme)
Part III—Physical Sciences
CHEMISTRY—Paper II

Time : 3 Hrs. Max. Marks : 60

Read the following instructions carefully;

1. All questions are compulsory.
2. Questions from Sl. Nos. 1to 18 are of "Very Short" answer type. Each question carries one mark. Every answer may be limited to a word, phrase or a sentence. Answer these questions continuously one after the other in the same serial order. Otherwise they will not be valued.
3. Questions from Sl. Nos. 19 to 28 are of "Short" answer type. Each question carries 3 marks. Every answer may be limited to 50 to 60 words.
4. Questions with serial Nos. 29 and 30 are of "Long" answer type. Each question carries 6 marks. Every answer may be limited to 250 words.

I

1. What is Nitrolium ?
2. Indicate the formula of Hypo.
3. Give the oxidation state of chlorine in perchloric acid.
4. Name the metal with highest percentage of composition in german silver.
5. What is molarity ?
6. How many electrons are present in the outer orbit of phosphorous in phosphorous pentachloride ?
7. Give the name of the product remains when sugar is heated with conc H_2SO_4.
8. Name the gas that is formed when potassium bromide reacts with fluorine.
9. What is the value of n if the outer electronic configuration of the first series of transition elements is $(n - 1)\ d^{1-10}\ ns^2$?
10. $NaOH\ (aq) + HCl\ (aq) \longrightarrow NaCl\ (aq) + H_20$

    What is known as the change of enthalpy in this reaction ?
11. At what temp. 80% of Ammonia is produced by Haber's process ?

12. Name the catalyst used in the manufacture of Sulphur trioxide by contact process.
13. Name the product when Ethylene undergoes ozonolysis.
14. Write the structure of 2, 2, 4 trimethyl pentane.
15. Indicate the factor which influences the equilibrium constant.
16. Give equation indicating how Ethane is prepared from Grignard Reagent.
17 When an alcohol reacts with a compound A it gives a product having a fruity odour. Name the functional group in the compound A.
18 What is the substance formed when Aniline is warmed with choloroform and alcohlic potash ?

II

19. Explain why N_2O_4 is colourless while NO2 is a reddish brown gas.
20. Explain why H_2O is a liquid while H_2S is a gas.
21. Give a neat and labelled diagram of Nelson's cell used in the manufacture of chlorine.
22. Calculate the weight of KOH present in 250ml. of 0.1 M potassium hydroxide solution.
23. Explain the nature of aqueous solution of Ammonium chloride.
24. Calculate the pH of 0.001 M HCl.
25. Calculate how many coulombs of electricity is needed to deposit 54g. of silver on cathode from silver nitrate solution.
26. Explain Hess law.
27. Explain the effect of Temp. and Pressure on the following equilibrium based on Le-Chatelier's principle

$$N_2 + 3H_2 \rightleftharpoons 2NH_3 + 22 \text{ K.cals.}$$

28. Explain Wurtz reaction with equation.

III

29. Name two important ores of zinc and give their formulae. Describe th extraction of zinc from zinc blend. Give equations.

OR

Explain the following :

a) Calcination b) Smelting c) Alumino thermic process

30. Give two methods of preparation of Acetone with equations. How can the following are prepared from Acetone and give equations.

a) Isopropyl alcohol b) Acetone oxime

OR

Give two methods of preparation of Acetic Acid with equations. How can the following are prepared from Acetic acid and give equations :

a) Acetyl Chloride b) Acetamide

Scientific and Technological Developments in India

Period	*Developments*	*Other Details*
150000-25000 B.C.	The Early stone Age (Early Palaeolithic)—Chopper-chopping tool culture.	The Punjab, Peninsular India (excepting extreme south India)
25000-5000 B.C.	The Middle Stone Age (Middle Palaeolithic)—Predominance of flake tools, scrappers, points, borers, etc.	The Punjab, Peninsular India (excepting extreme south India)
5000-3000 B.C.	The Late Stone Age (Mesolithic—Predominance of microliths, flakes, blades, lunates, scrappers, borers, chisels, triangles, trapezoids, drills, etc.	Gujarat, Madya Pradesh, Maharashtra, Mysore, Tamil Nadu (Tinnevelly) and West Bengal (Birbanpur), etc.
3500 B.C.	Neolithic Age	Baluchistan
2300-1750 B.C.	Harappan culture—Copper-bronze technology *cire perdue* method; wheell-made; decorated and glazed pottery; settled agriculture wheat and barley, domestication of animals; drainage and bath, burnt brick and mortar constructions; grid system of town planning; spinning and weaving; measurement and computational techniques.	Baluchistan, Sind, Punjab, Rajputana and Seurashtra
2000 B.C.	Some Neolithic settlements; agriculture; cave-drawing and paintings, depictings animals; handmade and wheel-made pottery.	Andhra, Karnatak, Bengal and Kashmir
1800 B.C.	Some Chalcolithic settlements; use of copper tools; Black/Red Ware; Malwa ware and Jarwe ware; spouted vessels.	Saurashtra, Rajputana, central, southern and eastern India

Period	*Developments*	*Other Details*
1800-1000 B.C.	Ochre-coloured ware—copperhoards.	Closed casting of metals
1500 B.C.	The *Rigveda*—concept of natural law; monistic idea concerning water; the *naksatra* system (lunar mansions) of marking ecliptic, beginnings of calender system; knowledge of diseases and cure; agricultural practices, use of plough, wheat and barley; fermentation methods; use of horse.	Earliest literary Composition; Punjab and *Kashmir regions*
1000 B.C.	The *Yajurveda*—series of 27 or 28 *naksatras* headed by *Krittika*, number names on the decimal scale up to 10^{12}; agricultural practices, mentioning of rice.	Western Uttar Pradesh
1000 B.C.	The *Athai ..uveda*—astronomical knowledge; details of *naksatras*, method of intercalation; details of medical knowledge and practices; lists of different plants and animal.	Concept of *prana* as the sustainer of life; some parts of *Atharveveda* seem to be earlier
1000-600 B.C.	The *Brahmanas, Aranyakas* and *Upanisads*—astronomical ideas, cosmic cycle; beginnings of mathematical series (A.P. and G.P.); more anatomical and physiological knowledge; doctrine of *pancabhutas*; more elucidation of the world of the living and non-living.	These ideas later influenced the Greeks
	Painted-Grey ware—in association with iron.	A deluxe pottery mainly mainly in northern and north-western parts of India
	Production and use of Iron.	In small open-hearth furnaces

Period	Developments	Other Details
	Agricultural practices—rotation following method to increase the soil fertility.	
600-400 B.C.	Northern Black-Polished ware, associated with the use of iron; making of stee..	Mainly in Eastern India; later spread to other parts of India
	Glass objects at Taxila.	Bhir mound at Taxila.
	Codification of medical knowledge into the *Ayurveda*.	
	Vedanga Jyotisa—five-year cycle; further elaboration of calendarical knowledge.	*Naksatra* system continued to be the basis.
	Sulba-sutras—beginnings of Geometry; anticipation of Pythagorean theorem; development of irrational-numbers' knowledge.	As aid to construction of sacrificial altars
	Early ideas of *Vaisesika; Samkhya* and Mimamasa, of the Budha, Jaina and the Carvaka; Physical concepts; atomism, space, time motion, sound.	As part of the religio-philosophical position.
400 B.C. —400 A.D.	The *Ayurvedic* treatises—the Caraka and Susruta *Samhitas*, containing the *tridosa* theory, physiology, anatomy, pathology, therapeutics and surgical practices.	Emphasis on herbal medicine; skill in lapa-ratomy, lithotomy and rhinoplasty
	Development of the orthodox philosophical sutras; the Jaina, the Budha schools; extension of the doctrines of five elements, space, time and sound.	Respective epistemological positions made specific.
	The *Arthasastra* of Kautilya; mining, metal working, agriculture and irrigation.	
	Bhagvati-sutra; Tattvarthadhigamahsutra of Umasvati· atomisms, classification of living and non-living.	

Period	Developments	Other Details
	Restatements of astronomical ideas; adoption of zodiacal system; knowledge of the motion of planets.	May be Greek or Babylonian influences
	Progress in mathematics; permutations and combinations—*meruprastrara* and the early binomial ideas.	Pingala's *Chandah-Sutra*
	Widespread use of iron; construction of Sudarsana Lake.	Use of bellows in extracting iron.
	Glass objects at a number of places	Foreign influences—Roman, at Taxila and Tamilnadu
A.D. 400–500	*Nyayabhasya* of Vatsyana—atomicism further extended; views on vision and propagation of sound; classification of animals and plants; impetus theory.	
	Padarthadhamasamgraha of Prasastapada; atomism; time, space, motion, sound	An independent work resembling vaisesika categories.
A.D. 400–500	*Aryabhatya*—Theory of the rotation of the earth, epicyclic theory for planetary motion; values of sines pie π; alphabetical system of expressing decimal place-value notation; interminate equation of the first order; extraction of square and cube roots.	Growth of the Indian decimal pleace-value system
	Metal workings; art of jewellery; Iron pillar now near Kutab Minar, Delhi.	Made of Wrought iron (99.72 %)
	Copper statue of Budha from Sultanganj, Bihar (now in Birmingham Musuem)	Cast in two layers
	Sophisticated ceramic ware.	On the Indo-Gangetic plains

Period	*Developments*	*Other Details*
A.D. 500–600	*Panchasiddhantika* of Varahamihira: the five Siddhantas —*Saura, Paulisa, Romaka. Brahma* and *Paitamaha*; concept of mahayuga (4,320,000 years); equinoxes in the *Suryasiddhanta.*	The *Suryasiddanta* emerged as the best and the most accurate
	Brhat Samhita of Varahamihira—Chemical processes; plant and animal classifications.	Encyclopaedic work
	Amarakosa—Classification and synonyms of plants and animlas, mineral and metals.	Lexicon
	Buddhist logic and Jaina views.	Problems of matter elucidated.
A.D. 600–800	Bramagupta (Astronomer and mathematician)—*Brahamasphutasiddhanta* and *Khandokhadyaka;* Lemma for solution of the interminate second order equation; formula for the sum of nth terms of A.P.; rules for the area of cyclic quadilateral and for the volume of a prism, etc.	Both translated into Arabic in the 8th century A.D., and named as *Sindhind* and *Arkand*
	Nyaya-vartika and Udyotakara; more elucidation of atomic views.	
	Rugvinscaya of Madhava; diagnostic methods.	Also called *Madhavanidana;* translated as Arabic and titled as *Badon*
	Astangahrdaya of Vagbhata—an authoritative compilation of the Ayurvedic knowledge based on the early works.	Changed in Arabic and titled as *Astankar*
A.D. 800–1000	*Ganitasarasamgraha* of Mahavira : Operations involving zero and Summation of n terms of G.P	Mysore

Period	Developments	Other Details
	Krsi-Parasara and *Vrksayurveda*.	Manuals on agriculture and botany.
	Alchemical practices; *Rasahrdaya* of Govinda Bhagavat.	As part of tantrik prapractic
	Siddha system of medicine.	Tamilnadu; mainly mineral medicinés.
	Munjala's elucidation about procession of equinoxes	In competition with earlier libration concept
A.D. 1000–1200	Sridhara's method of solving quadratic equations.	
	Siddhantasironani of Bhaskara II : astronomical and mathematical work in four parts; *cakravala* method for rational integral solutions of the indeterminate equation of the second order; geometric proof of the Pythagorean theorem; root idea of differential calculas; elaboration of epicyclic-eccentric theories for planetary motions; analysis of the motion of the sun by considering longitudinal changes.	Influenced later astronomers and mathematicians; some commentaries followed; represents the height of Indian mathematics and astronomy
	Manasollasa of Somadeva; alchemy; perfumery; iron-casting.	
	Knowledge of paper-making	Came possibly from Nepal and Arabia.
A.D. 1200–1500	*Sarangdhara Samahita*—opium and its materia medica, pulse and urine examination for diagnosis.	Foreign influences
	Rasasastra texts : *Rasarnava*, *Resaratnakara; Resaratnasamuccaya* etc.; classification of substances; experimental techniques.	Skill in Chemical processes

Period	Developments	Other Details
	Narayana Pandita—further refinement of arithmatic and algebraic operations.	
	Paramesvara—commentator on astronomical and mathematical works Pyrothechnics.	Belonged to Kerala. Production Centres in South India
A.D. 1500–1600	*Ganesa Daivajna*—commentator on astronomical and mathematical works.	Maharashtra
	Use of mercurial and non-mercurial compositions in medicines; *Bhavaprakasa :* materia medica, treatment of syphilis; Gunpowder and guns.	Largely used during the Mughal period.
	Advent of the Portuguese physician Garcia da orta, introduction of new economic plants.	Publication of Garcia's Colloquies (1565)
A.D. 1600–1700	*Tuzuk-i-Jahangiri*—about animals and plants. Advent of the Dutch, French and the British, study of Indian flora.	Commercialization
1723–27	Construction of Jantar Mantars at Delhi, Ujjain, Mathura, Banaras, Jaipur by Maharaja Sawai Jai Singh II.	Huge masonry astronomical instruments
	Samrat Siddhanta of Jaganatha.	Translation of the Arabic version of Ptolemy's *Almagest*
	Rekhaganita of Jaganatha.	Translation of the Arabic version of Euclid's *The Elements*
1737	d' Anville's first map of South India, his map of India, *carte de l' Inde*.	Based on Maragha school of astronomy and Jesuit sources.
1755	Botanical investigation of Koenig in South India.	The collection was sent to the University of Lund in Sweden.

Period	Developments	Other Details
1764	Ganges river course Surveyed by Rennell	Organized by East India Company.
1781	Madrasah at Calcutta.	Established on the initiative of Warren Hastings.
1783	First Map of Hindoostan by Rennel	
1784	The Asiatic Society founded at Calcutta.	The Founder President was William James.
1785	First paper (in Persian) presented with title—The care of the Elephantiasis and other Disorder of the Blood.	Translated and presented by William Jones himself
1787	Royal Botanic Garden at Sibpur, Calcutta.	Robert Kyd (first Honorary Superintendent
1791	*Samskrta Pathasala* at Banaras.	By the efforts of Janathan Duncan
1792	Madras Observatory established.	By Michael Topping
1794	Survey School at Madras.	Beginnings of trigonometrical Survey.
1795	Commencement of the publication of the *Flora Indica*.	Three volumes in 1795, 1802 and 1819
1800	Establishment of Trigonometrical Survey Department at Madras.	
1813	Introduction of a clause (in East India Company's Charter) for spending on *lac* rupees per year for the promotion of knowledge of sciences among people of India.	Beginning of British interests in educating the Indians in Science.
1817	Establishment of Mahavidyalaya (Hindu College) at Calcutta.	Public patronage of English education.
1822	Preparation of the Atlas of India on the quarter inch scale.	

Period	*Developments*	*Other Details*
1832	Publication of *Journal of the Asiatic Society* of Bengal.	
1835	Calcutta Medical College.	
1843	Medical School at Madras	
1845	The Grant Medical School at Bombay.	
1847	Engineering Institution at Roorkee.	Later became Thomson Engineering College.
1851	Establishment of the Geological Survey of India.	Thomas Old ham's efforts.
1851	The first telegraph line between Calcutta and Diamond Harbour	By William O' Shaughnessy
1853	The first railway line laid.	Near Bombay.
1854	Charles Wood's Despatch for the creation of the Universities	On the model of the London University.
	Engineering School at Poona.	
1856	Engineering College at Sibpur, Calcutta.	
1857	Establishment of the first three Universities at Calcutta, Bombay and Madras.	Only affiliating and examining bodies
1859	Civil Engineering College at Madras.	
	Establishment of Archaeological Survey of India	Cunningham as the Archaelogical Surveyor
1867	Indian Museum came in to being at Calcutta.	Gallaries thrown open to public in 1878
1875	Establishment of India Meteorogical Department.	
1876	Foundation of the Indian Association for the Cultivation of Science.	By Mahendra Lal Sircar through public endowments.
1881	Publication of the first mathematical paper of Asutosh Mukherji.	In the *Messenger of Mathematics*

Period	*Developments*	*Other Details*
1884	Centenary of the Asiatic Society of Bengal; papers published—500 in mathematical and physical sciences, 560 in Zoology, 320 in Botany.	Calcutta
1890	Imperial Bacteriological Laboratory at Poona.	Shifted in 1893 to Mukteswar
	Botanical Survey of India formed.	George King appointed as the frist Director
1895	Foundation of Solar Physics Laboratory at Kodaikanal.	Working started in 1900
	J.C. Bose's first scientific paper on the polarization of electric waves by double refraction.	Published in JASB
1896	Plague Research Laboratory at Bombay, whose name was changed (in 1906) to Haffkine Institute.	Haffkine was appointed as the first Director
	P.C. Ray's work on mercurous compounds.	Published in JASB
	Recommendation of the Royal Agricultural Commission emphasized research on agriculture.	Establishment of Imperial Agricultural Research Institue at Pusa (Bihar), in 1903.
1897	J.C. Bose's lecture at the Royal Institute, London, with his own apparatus, the Electric Radiator. He preceded Marconi in discovering Wireless Telegraphy.	
1900	J.C. Bose's paper, 'On the Generality of the Molecular Phenomena produced by Electricity on Living and Non-living substances.'	Paper was read at the International Congress in Physics at Paris
	P.C. Ray's analysis of a number of rare Indian mine-	Published in the Memoirs of the Geological

Period	*Developments*	*Other Details*
	rals to discover in them some of the missing elements in Mendeleef's Periodic Table.	Survey of India
1914	Indian Science Congress Association formed with the Hon'ble Justice Sir Asutosh Mookherjee as its first President.	Calcutta
	J.C. Bose designed High Magnification Crescograph to measure slow growth rate of plants, which earned him FRS in 1920.	
1914–1919	S. Ramanujan (FRS, 1918) published 21 research papers and solved many intricate mathematical problems such as partitioning of natural numbers and solution of the famous Waring Problem.	University of Cambridge
1917	Meghnad Saha (FRS, 1927) gave Theory of Thermal Ionisation; Epoch-making Saha's equation for degree of ionisation in a stellar atmosphere.	
1930	Sir C.V. Raman became the first Asian Nobel Laureate in Physics.	For his discovery *Raman effect* and *Raman Spectra*
1935	National Institute of sciences formed which was later renamed as INSA.	Delhi
1936	Birbal Sahni (FRS, 1936) pioneering work in Indian Palaeobotany. He was elected President of the International Botanical Congress, Stockholm, 1950.	Lucknow
1940	CSIR formed with S.S. Bhatnagar (FRS, 1943) as its Founder Director.	

Period	*Developments*	*Other Details*
1941	H.J. Bhabha (FRS, 1941) gave Casacade Theory of cosmic-ray showers, and Vertor Theory of Meson.	
	Establishment of TIFR.	Bombay
	Establishment of Atomic Energy Establishment, which was later renamed as BARC.	Trombay
	Atomic Reactors Commissioned	Cirus, Rajasthan and Tarapur.
1950	Establishment of National Physical Laboratory.	New Delhi
1958	S.N. Bose (FRS, 1958) work in Nuclear Physics got international fame. Bose-Einstein statistics has become an integral part of text-books on modern physics. All nuclear elementary particles are now categorised—*Bosons* and *Fermions*.	
1965	India developed the process for the manufacture of optical glass which is a closely guarded secret of about ten countries in the world, under the guidance of Dr. Atma Ram (who pioneered Glass Technology in India). He is the first Asian to become Honorary Fellow of the Society of Glass Technology, Sheffield.	
1971	M.S. Swaminathan (FRS, 1973) got Ramon Mogsaysay Award for Community Leadership and recognized as 'Scientist, educator and administrator towards generating a new confidence in India's agricultural capabilities. He has been the key figure in bringing the Green Revolution in Asia.	
1974	India's first peaceful nuclear explosion (under the guidance of Dr. Raja Ramanna).	Pokharan

Period	*Developments*	*Other Details*
1975	India stood the forth among the countries that supplied experts (538) to the United Nations Development Programme (1975).	
1980	By the end of 1980, the number of Indian scientists who have been honoured with FRS, has come around forty.	
Later......	India has developed missile technology.	
	Now we are launching indegeneously developed satellites in the space.	
	Rockets to launch satellites are reaching to success.	
	One of the world leaders in space technology.	
	Successfully achieved the white revolution and blue revolution.	
	Exporters of certain technologies.	
	Became master brains in computer science. Developed our own super computer.	
	Extending assistance to many developed and developing nations on various earch sciences.	
	Main supplier of human resources to world countries in the fields of medicine, engineering, technology, agriculture, etc.	
	Paved way to industrial revolution.	
	Many scientists are working in many international commissions as specialists.	
	More than 200 universities having nearly 30,000 affiliated colleges are striving for quality education and research.